Harry Jones

East and West London

Being notes of common life and pastoral work in Saint James's, Westminster, and in

Saint George's-in-the-East

Harry Jones

East and West London
Being notes of common life and pastoral work in Saint James's, Westminster, and in Saint George's-in-the-East

ISBN/EAN: 9783337336325

Printed in Europe, USA, Canada, Australia, Japan

Cover: Foto ©ninafisch / pixelio.de

More available books at **www.hansebooks.com**

EAST AND WEST LONDON

BEING NOTES OF COMMON LIFE AND

PASTORAL WORK IN SAINT JAMES'S, WESTMINSTER

AND IN SAINT GEORGE'S-IN-THE-EAST

BY THE

REV. HARRY JONES, M.A.

RECTOR OF SAINT GEORGE'S-IN-THE-EAST

LONDON

SMITH, ELDER, & CO., 15 WATERLOO PLACE

1875

PREFACE.

I HAVE penned most of this little volume at odd times in the course of a very busy year, and finished it in my holydays ; but, however short it may come of my wishes and its title, it is at any rate no mere hasty utterance.

I have tried to set plainly down something of what I have seen, and some of the conclusions to which I have been led, during a ministry of twenty-five years in several parts of London. Thus, whether I have learned aright from it or not, at least I speak from experience.

As, however, the chief matters of which I write, such as pastoral economy, education, and sanitary or social improvements, are neither new nor of themselves necessarily entertaining, I have not scrupled to garnish them with some touches of natural life that have happened to come in my way ; for I want my little book to be read, and not thrown aside as a mere dull contribution to the large store of current published opinions on questions of a civil and ecclesiastical character.

I have written it with deep interest in the grave subjects of which it mainly treats, and I hope to engage the sympathy of those who are anywise concerned in promoting the welfare of their fellows, and, though they may occasionally differ from him, are willing to hear what a man of some experience has to say about matters which no thoughtful worker, or well-wisher of his kind, regards with indifference.

I may add that, in speaking about various modes of Church work, I have been conscious of a desire to avoid strictly theological questions, and I hope I have successfully resisted that tendency to sermonise, with which we parsons are sometimes credited, when we talk of things with which we are continuously and professionally occupied.

In respect of divers facts referred to in the following pages, I have avoided any display of statistics. For some details in the latter part of the Chapter on Trades and Industries, I have used information supplied in a series of interesting articles on these matters now being published in the *East London Observer.* I enter on no archæological or historical ground, and chiefly confine myself to those characteristics of current social life and pastoral work in the East and West of London which have come under my own observation.

HARRY JONES.

RECTORY, ST. GEORGE'S IN THE EAST:
October, 1875.

CONTENTS.

EAST AND WEST LONDON.

INTRODUCTORY.

I DIP my pen to write the first line of this book with a consciousness that it must be rather egoistic if written at all.

It is a rough impression of my own experience and opinions; and, do what I will, I cannot help using a large number of capital I's in its compilation. The subject is one which ought especially to interest Londoners; and as I have been repeatedly asked about it by friends, I fancy that some others may care to read what is at least an honest record of personal observation.

Circumstances led me some two years ago to move from a populous Western district of which I had long had charge—that of St. Luke's, Berwick Street, in St. James's, Westminster—to St. George's in the East, a large parish lying a little beyond the Tower, and containing the London Docks.

B

Thus I have the opportunity of bringing the experience of many years in the West to the observation of the East.

The result hitherto has been the correction of much of my own ignorance and the dissipation of some prejudice. As soon as I came I began in an aimless sort of way, sometimes even as I walked along the street, jotting down impressions on scraps of paper, just as they occurred, without any order or connection, and stuffing them into a large envelope. This has now grown ready to burst, and after emptying the heap of pencil notes upon my study table I have tried to assimilate and reproduce them. I cannot, however, transform this papery jumble into a severely connected record. Thus, if any one cares to be my reader, I must ask him to forgive me for the discursive and colloquial shape of my attempt ; for, after all, I must offer the fruit of my observation much as it was gathered.

My first impression was, perhaps, of the nearness of the East of London to the West. The East is, to many who dwell in the West, an unknown distant land. Anything beyond the City is indefinitely remote. I lived close to the Langham Hotel, and on the occasion of my first taking Sunday duty at St. George's I hailed a crawling cab in Portland Place and drove there. To my surprise it landed me at the gate of my new church in twenty-eight minutes. Of course, it being Sunday, the streets were clear, but I had not urged the driver to any special speed. The next week I got the jailor at the Marlborough Street police-court to go over my course with the fatal wheel which decides the disputes between cabmen and their 'fares.' The distance from the Oxford Street Circus to the iron gate of the church at St. George's in the East turned out to be something under four miles—a verdict which several cabmen have since heard with much professional affectation of scepticism; but on my informing them of my authority they have shown by their acquiescence that they had drawn upon their faith in the vaguely exaggerated public conceptions of the remoteness of the East in attempting to decline half-a-crown for the journey.

It is not, however, the actual distance so much

as the throng in the City which divides the East of
London from the West.

By day Westminster and Whitechapel are, so
to speak, on the opposite sides of a thick wood;
but at night, or when the road is clear, they are
easily joined by a half-hour's drive. The railways,
from whichever side they approach it, as yet only
empty themselves into the rim round the centre of
London; and thus they have hitherto done little
toward bringing the suburbs together. Wherever
you alight there is the same dense core to be
penetrated and passed through before an opposite
terminus can be reached. Presently, however,
there will be one connecting line between at least
the East and West.

The East London Railway, which runs through
the old Thames Tunnel and is burrowing under
the London Docks, will, by striking into the Great
Eastern Low Level, meet the extension of the
Metropolitan at Liverpool Street, and thus provide
a new way through part of the parishes of Bethnal
Green, Stepney, and St. George's in the East, from
Paddington to the Sydenham district, and so on to
Brighton. This will of course immensely benefit

us Easterners. Now we have no wholly unimpeded road westward but the river. This in summer-time provides a cheap and pleasant access to Westminster by the Greenwich boats which call at various piers above the Tower.

After all, however, the East is very much farther from the West than the West is from the East.

When I lived near the line of Regent Street, I intended for years to make an expedition to the Ratcliff Highway ; but I was deterred, I imagine, chiefly by the supposed length of the trip. Now that I live near the Highway I find that I can get easily, by three or four routes, to my old neighbourhood in from half an hour to forty-five minutes.

The second general impression I received of the East of London was in respect to its spaciousness. Anyone may perceive this who penetrates and then traverses the City from the West, and after passing the 'Butcher's Row' at Aldgate enters on either of the broad thoroughfares, traversed by trams, which are called the Commercial Road or the Mile End Road. These, shortly after leaving the City, become two of the widest streets in London, and the pavement in the Mile End Road in particular is proportionately as wide as the roadway.

They are characteristic of the East, and branching off from them on either side may be seen long tributaries of modest houses, many, I may say most of them, only two stories high, in which rent is low and where the tenants get plenty of elbow-room.

The Mile End Road dies out into the country —which, by the way, involves Epping Forest—with a growing fringe of villas; and the Commercial Road justifies its name more and more as it goes on and reveals, by the masts of the ships in the docks, its connection with the maritime commerce of London.

To recur to that part of the East which is daily before me, and which lies immediately on the right of the Commercial Road after passing Whitechapel. It eminently impresses me with the sense of spaciousness. In this my present parish presents a remarkable contrast to the district in which I had worked for some years. There my church was jammed up so tightly in the centre of a crowd of courts that a stranger walking down

Berwick Street, at the bottom of which it was placed, might traverse nearly the whole street and come away without suspecting that it contained a church at all.

Here the church dominates—in a material sense—the whole parish, and has a disused church-yard of some three acres at its foot, or, rather, heel. There, at St. Luke's, we had a densely crowded population. That of the Berwick Street division of St. James's, Westminster, has been stated in published statistics to be the most crowded in the metropolis. My reader may believe me or not, but I am speaking the truth when I tell him that we had 10,000 people in 300 yards square. Here the streets are wider, the houses are less closely packed together, and poor people especially have more room. There, an artisan in the receipt of good wages is frequently obliged to content himself with one apartment, which serves for all purposes, and for which he pays some five or six shillings a-week. Here he can get a whole house of four rooms, with a commodious yard at its back, for about the same sum.

Many people entertain a vaguely erroneous

idea of the crowded 'slums' of the East.   For the worst or most frequent specimens of 'slums' they should go to some parts of central London, or even some portions of St. James's, Westminster, and its contiguous parishes.   Of course there are not a few vile corners and courts in the East ; but, on the whole, the working classes are much better lodged here at St. George's than in those parts of the West of which I know most.   And our neighbouring parishes of Stepney and Limehouse have fewer crowded corners than we have.   Then, too—I speak of the districts which skirt the river—an enormous sense of space is afforded by the docks.   These give us, moreover, something beyond a sense of space—a touch of catholicity or cosmopolitanism which is hard to be defined, though very real.   It was a new sensation to me when walking down a street to see its whole width gradually filled up by, say, a full-rigged tea-ship from China, which, after months of plunging in tropical seas, was now creeping through the last few yards of its progress to some calmest nook within the docks, and, like a monster vessel in a play, crossed the stage silently with even keel.

All sorts of ships thus traverse St. George's, and, as may be supposed, contribute to the stream in its streets as well as to the crowd in its waters. You hear many languages on its pavements, and see men in all colours of skin and dress. This passing contact and contrast of races, this mixture of land and water, of homely trucks and foreign traders, of horse-vans and steam-vessels ; the tier of huge ocean-going ships, brought so close to the shore that you can touch their long black sides with your stick or umbrella as you pace the edge of the docks, produces that sentiment of proximity to the ends of the world of which I have spoken, and which adds to the sense of space that characterises this part of the East of London. And I must remark, in passing, that this evidence of relationship with other parts of the earth seems to me to have its effect on the wits of the residents in St. George's.

Education has been somewhat neglected here—more of this presently—but the people are, it strikes me, eminently shrewd and colloquially intelligent. Their acquaintance with distant commerce must, I think, account for a certain freedom from that local exclusiveness of sentiment and information which characterises many dense communities. Fresh points are given to the many-sided sharpness of London life by familiarity with distant interests.

Another phase of spaciousness appears in the interest which many of the working classes here take in the keeping of animals. I do not now refer to Mr. Jamrach, whose beasts are my parishioners—though the fact of St. George's being notoriously the central market of the world for lions, bears, tigers, elephants, monkeys, and parrots, must create a sentiment of cosmopolitanism among those who can hear them howl and chatter —but to tamer tastes, exhibited in the possession of pigeons, fowls, and dogs. I appreciated the opportunities for this myself, and, being fond of most live things, soon had a company of cocks and hens, which resulted in abundance of fresh eggs throughout the year.

One of my fowls, born at St. George's, exhibited such a curious phase of human appreciation as to be worth record. He liked to be 'patted.' I had only to open the glass door of the parlour, which looks on the churchyard, and call 'Pip'—he answered to his name—and Pip ran up from among his colleagues to be thus coaxed. I used to feed him with corn kept in a certain cupboard in my entrance. Pip knew the cupboard well, and when he could make his way into the house used to plant himself before it in an attitude of anticipation. But this fowl suffered from the precocity of genius; he overdrew the resources of his brain. As he grew to full estate he lost much of his confidence in me, though I had done nothing to deserve the loss of it. And now, an adult and gaudy cock, though he likes corn as much as ever, he is the most nervous of the whole plumed assemblage when they present themselves under my dining-room window at breakfast-time to be fed. Perhaps he suffers from a suspicion of the uncertainty of his place in the community, for his father—a tough old gentleman, who once, with great applause, though after strenuous conflict, beat off a game-cock who invaded his harem—takes every opportunity of snubbing his son. And Pip's spirit has shrunk while his body has grown. He has become a 'Toots' in his society. Gaily dressed, and with amiable disposition, he has failed in mental

development, and is in consequence proportionately underrated.

I must here, too, introduce a line about my
dogs. First came, a present from a friend—'Jem,'
half Newfoundland and half retriever, coal black,
and endued with more capacity for heating himself
in the sun than any dog I ever knew. His back,
he is aware, will get warm by simple exposure;
but he bakes his lower half, which is necessarily in
partial shade, by straddling out his legs like an
heraldic eagle, and effecting an abdominal contact
with the hot stones. He delights neither to bark
nor bite. Selim-ben-Guy, a noble deer-hound
(likewise a present) lays hold of Jem's tail and drags
his good-natured carcase about backwards, like
a black sledge, without more than a feeble remonstrance when Guy takes a fresh purchase with
those tremendous teeth of his. I am afraid, however,
of keeping Guy in London, so he mostly sojourns
in the country, and pays us or receives an occasional
visit.

Not so with 'Nep,' whom I got in this wise.
I called him 'Nep,' after trying over name after
name with him and finding that he answered to this.

One day I was returning from Charing Cross by the steamboat, and saw in the bows a lovely brown web-footed retriever, with a tarline round his neck, in the custody of two or three roughs, who said aloud and incidentally that they had fished him out of the river as he was being carried down by the tide.

Nep caught my eye, and looked at me with such a petitioning glance that I went up and spoke to him. If ever dog replied, he begged me to take him home. I remarked, half to myself, knowing that it is famous for its brown retrievers, ' That dog came from Maldon in Essex.' Nep's keepers understood me, I suppose (I didn't think of it till afterwards) to claim the knowledge, not of his breed, but of his owner's address, and promptly replied, ' If the gentleman will give us half-a-crown for finding him he shall have him." So I tendered the half-crown, with the condition that they should let me have the tarline too, and led him off when we touched at the Thames Tunnel Pier, which is our landing-place at St. George's. But he wanted no leading. At once, and permanently, he accepted me as his master, and—I having failed to discover his owner—remains the sharpest of house dogs. His passion, though, for the water, exceeds that of any water dog I ever possessed. I took him down for some time into the country, where there was a large shallow muddy pond. All day long Nep busied himself in ploughing the bottom of it with his nose, and bringing ashore every stone and saturated stick he thus discovered, till the pool had quite a fringe of these rescued treasures. Of course this procedure kept Nep's face shamefully dirty, and had to be prohibited. He will, however, 'tub' himself, though with an eye to the sensation of being wet rather than to that of cleanliness. He gets with all his four legs into a tub of water, and ducks his head under it, then he splashes himself with his fore paws. But he does not seem to know how to wet his back. Nep once lost himself in the streets of St. George's, and in the course of his rounds came upon the river. I had given him up for lost, when one Sunday a smiling policeman brought him back in custody. He had my name on his collar—not the constable, but the dog—and from 'information received' I gathered he had been for four days accepting the civilities of young mud-larks or shore-boys, who had incessantly thrown sticks in the water for him during that period. He seemed to have eaten nothing, being as lean as a basket, and was wet to the bone; but the temptation had been too much for him. He had tasted a Paradise of splashes, and thought of nothing else. Nep thinks, however. When the first frost came this last winter, his pan of water was slightly frozen. Nep, finding his thirsty nose mystically repelled, at once stepped back and broke the ice with a blow of his right paw. He is completely the master of Jem, and would chastise Selim-ben-Guy, when troublesome, if he could catch him. Jem somehow soon infringed, unawares, the limits of that armed neutrality exhibited between dogs when they first meet; and Nep, though much less in size, tumbled him about in the churchyard like a kitten, and made him lift up his voice and cry, even when he had done with him. In fact, after this unexpectedly brisk introduction, Jem went off and blubbered by himself among the tombstones on the north side of the church. Guy sometimes cannot resist trying a sudden haul at Nep's tail, which is attractively bushy, and offers an excellent grip ; but on Nep's resenting this liberty, which he always does, and furiously, shows him his heels in a frolicsome circuitous gallop, intended to be construed as part of the game. Nep meanwhile hunts him angrily, though hopelessly, till he is tired, Guy throughout insisting on looking upon the whole affair as a joke, enjoyed equally by both parties. But Nep does not see it.

I hope my readers will forgive this digression. It is, however, illustrative of the sense of space which impressed me on going to what is loosely reckoned by some as one of the densely crowded and dull districts in London.

There is a sentiment of elbow-room and' manifold life at St. George's which is felt and reflected by its natives. Not that they do not work, and work hard. No one can live in the East without perceiving this. Life has a very severe and importunate side in these parts. The air is heavily charged with the sentiment of toil, and there is little to stir it. We seem not only to be always at work, but we hardly ever have a glimpse of the unoccupied side of London life. Every one appears either to have something to do or to be seeking work. I except, of course, the phase of relaxation, often grossly offensive, exhibited by sailors ashore, who crowd as much coarse indulgence as possible into the few hours at their disposal. Otherwise, all are obviously about some business. No one dreams of a carriage airing in this part of the East. Here I have never seen a coachman in a wig, or a footman in powder. I have never met a lady on horseback, or a 'Victoria;' and, though we go much about on foot, such a luxury as a crossing-sweeper is unknown. I tax my memory but I do not recollect ever to have seen a 'Punch' at St. George's. As I think about it I perceive that here the strain of work and sentiment of toil is continuous. It is unbroken by the exhibition of equipages and pleasure seekers that marks the 'London Season.' Here our only 'seasons' are summer and winter. We are hot or cold, but we are always at work. September is marked by no difference in the aspect of our streets. We have no fixed busy time, for all times are the same. We do not know when London is 'full' or 'empty,' when Parliament meets or disperses. The only annual event which makes a distinct impression on the neighbourhood is the Cambridge and Oxford boat-race. Then the smallest little draper's shop down the loneliest and dullest street breaks out in blue ribands, and the van horses toiling up Old Gravel Lane from the Docks wear their colour. The papers tell those who please to read such information, of Gun Clubs, Polo Clubs, Four-in-Hand Gatherings, Lord's Cricket-matches, Garden Parties, Annual Exhibitions, and all the machinery of pleasure and play, whose wheels are set going from Easter till August, but no echo of this yearly stir reaches us here.

We live much from hand to mouth. Every farthing has to be earned, and a sixpence is severely perceived to be worth six pennies. True there is some pretext for relaxation associated with Victoria Park and the Bethnal Green Museum, but here we sorely want some mollifying influence, some commentary of ornament. The strain of toil is too importunate. An illustration of the general acceptance of the prevailing necessity of work in these parts appears in the use that is made of the big bell of our church—a use of it which, I fancy, would not be tolerated in the West of London.

The parish is proud of its peal of bells. There are eight of them, and at a little distance, or on Sunday before service, they sound well; though practices and rehearsals fill every room, within the radius of some hundred yards or so, with a tremendous din. We have, too, a sonorous clock, which chimes the quarters and strikes the hours with a will. Besides ordinary marking of time by the clock, the curfew is regularly rung; and so is the morning alarum.

St. George's is the only place I know of in which the curfew fulfils some of its original purpose. Directly the clock has done striking eight it tolls for a quarter of an hour; and I am informed that it gives the signal for the cessation of work and the turning-off of the gas in divers workshops.

But the tolling of the day is preeminently in the morning. Then the big bell is rung for fifteen minutes before six, with irregular clang. Sometimes a few strokes are less vigorous than others, but they are never equidistant, and they are always strong. The purpose of this peal or metal monologue is not so much to herald the hour at which work should begin as to awaken the workers, and

as it has been so rung for years by the same man
he has become an expert in the business. The
sleeping ear might survive an even unvarying
sound, such as the striking of a clock, but it could
hardly outsleep the strain of our alarum.

Did Mr. Fleming, our awakener, toll the bell
with the same regularity and force as that which
announces the hour, I believe that many might
sleep through the summons, though he sounded it
for a quarter of an hour. It is remarkable how
soon the ear learns to accommodate itself to a
recurrent sound, when it is simply and evenly repeated. But Mr. Fleming knows better than merely
to reproduce his message. He never precisely re-
peats his morning performance ; sometimes he tolls
rapidly and loudly for a minute, then pausing for
some fifty seconds, he gives a couple of clangs
which seem to discharge an accumulated store of
sound. Then, after another silence, he lets off another big bang; to wait again during a parenthesis
which is broken by a score of strokes, that increase
in loudness, and crowd so closely on each other,
that one wonders how he can get the heavy clapper
to obey his tugs with sufficient rapidity. But his

great and expiring effort arrives when the chimes begin to precede the striking of six o'clock. Then, stimulated by the additional perception that he can produce a discord as well as a noise, he pulls with a will, and produces a tocsin so complicated and vehement, that if the sleeper has outslept even the summons of the previous fifteen minutes, he must awake, at least if he lives anywhere near the church. My house adjoins it. Its tower is so close that I can hear the rattle of the rope and the groan of the wheel before each metal 'boom.' And when the last stroke of six has been struck in a storm of accompanying clangour from the heavy alarum bell, the air long remains filled with an angry hum, as if the emperor of all the hornets was flying around the room.

And this is done summer and winter, wet and dry. No wonder, if I have not finally contracted a habit of early rising, that I frequently find myself in my study at six o'clock.

Here, in this tocsin, this alarum, which is meant to be intolerable, and so borne with, we have re-markable witness to the general acceptance of the necessity of work in these parts. A great feature of the business here is cartage. The goods brought into dock from over the seas are incessantly being dispersed by wheel and axle. When the tocsin ceases you presently begin to hear a dull, distant rumble of wheels as the vans start for their day's work.

Barring the bells, however, which really represent ' noise' only to those who live close to them, this, though a populous and busy part of London, is tolerably quiet. The rectory, which stands a little off the street, is remarkably free from the usual London noises. Though I can discern the dull grind of wheels down Cannon Street Road, most of our vehicles move slowly. They are heavily laden. There is hardly any of the sharp penetrating rattle which is made by swift carriages and cabs ; and the disturbance, lasting into the small hours of the morning, created by a contiguous late ' party' in the season is, of course, unknown.

The route of the Blackwall Railway, which traverses the parish, is distantly indicated by its whistles, but I hear little of the trains. Late at night, when the public-houses are emptied, there is an accession of shouts and singing, mostly from

sailors abusing their liberty ashore by getting more
or less drunk. But, curiously enough, to us this
clamour seems to come from the church, which
'corners' on the rectory. The west front of its
tower catches and reflects the noises that arise
from the street. When I first heard these I fancied
that some riotous party had made its way into the
churchyard, but I soon found that they were
strictly the echoes of that nocturnal dissipation
which may be heard everywhere in the neighbourhood of publicans, especially when they turn their
customers out of doors. There is another sound,
too, which is more constant in the evenings, and
which for a long time I could not make out. I
thought several times that somebody had upset a
chair or table in the next room but one. It was as
if a visitor was announcing his call by kicking in-
termittently at the outer gate with his shoes off.
At last I found that these dull thuds came from a
covered skittle-alley some fifty yards off. What I
heard was that from the successful shots of the
players. The sounds we hear are, however,
altogether less than what one might expect from
Ratcliff Highway. Most of the other streets are

usually quiet enough, the liquor houses being chiefly congregated in our main thoroughfares.

As to the street organs and bands which plague the West End, I cannot say that I have heard one while sitting indoors at St. George's. There are a few to be met with sometimes, but very few. I seem never to hear them. Nor is there anything like the commercial row which costermongers used to make under my windows a few yards from Portland Place. There they incessantly proceeded, two to a barrow, day after day, offering onions, rhubarb, what not, in a yell, hour after hour, without ever, as far as I could perceive, meeting with any response to their tremendous proposals. Here, too, we have no roaring liars or frozen-out gardeners.

Indeed, barring the bells, our chief household noises arise from our own cocks and hens, which record their domestic events with more cackling than I ever heard in connection with them. The vividness with which these are heard says much for the general quiet of our surroundings. When I am saying the daily morning service in the church hard by, I can distinctly note the advertisement of another egg.

Before I close this rambling introductory chapter, I am reminded by the last sentences, which recall the living animals about my house, that I may be pardoned for saying a word or two more concerning Nep and Selim-ben-Guy. I have been much exercised in observing their characters, which reveal such an amount of jealousy between them as I have never known dogs exhibit. They cannot agree long, do what I will, since each devours me with demands, not only for scraps, but for personal notice. Sometimes one will not come into the dining-room when he knows that the other is there, and when they are both present they occasionally snarl at each other so much so as to make their joint company and conversation undesirable.

Nep is a singular dog, with very marked individualities. He exhibits the extremes of affection and irascibility. If he is set to guard anything— say a pair of boots—woe be to anyone beside a recognised personage who should attempt to touch them. He will at least growl at anyone except a member of the household who enters the kitchen. With all this anxious attitude of defence or defiance, he brims with the uttermost joy on the recurrence of stated occasions. Every morning he repairs to my dressing-room with as boisterous a welcome as if I had been round the world and he had not seen me for a twelvemonth. He rushes upstairs with seemingly a hundred legs, and bursts into my room jumping with all four feet off the ground at the same time in a paroxysm of greeting. I never saw a dog so leap with excess of feeling. His saltations are varied with a gesture I never saw before in a dog. He comes to my feet and essays to lay his head under them. When he has performed this obeisance he trots about the room with the tread of a cob. At any time, however, if I say, ' Nep, abase yourself,' he submits his neck as if he wished it to be trodden on, and licks my boots.

He is an obstinate dog, though. One day I sent him with my servant to Victoria Park for a swim, and once in the water he would not come out. My man found, though, that this prolonged bath was forbidden by the police, and had to go to the police-station to answer for Nep's obstinacy. Meanwhile Nep swam about in the middle of the water till he was tired. He cannot bear cats or kittens, though he manages to confine his dislike to grinning and growling at them. In this he is wholly unlike Selim-ben-Guy, with whom they take all manner of liberties. I have one or two cats, and a succession of resultant kittens. Now, our senior churchwarden has been kind enough to give Guy a big round basket, in which he sleeps, and when he goes to bed his little friends coil themselves up in his indentations. In fact, he reposes 'levelled up' with kittens.

NOTE.—Since I have written this chapter a muffled peal has been rung for our chief bell-ringer, Mr. Fleming. I paid my last visit to him just before he died, and shall not soon forget the smile which lit up his old face when I went into his room. He died mainly of old age, and stuck to his duty till he was laid up in his bed. The last time he went up the winding turret stairs to pull his bell he had to sit down on the stone steps two or three times for breath. But he got into the belfry and tolled his parting curfew.

IN the course of this book I have necessarily perceived that if I set down my honest impressions I must not omit those concerning the Church and position of the clergy which I have received in reviewing and contrasting clerical work in the West and the East of London. And thus I may as well speak of these matters at once. But, as I am conscious of differing from some whose character and labours I respect, I approach this part of my subject, not with misgiving, but with that sense of possible exposure to unpleasant misapprehension which always accompanies the utterance of sentiments which are not sure to meet with general acceptance. This part of the subject is, however, in my judgment, the most important, and I must say my say at the risk of being mis-understood, and, in so far as I am fortunate in having clerical readers, being possibly censured by some of them.

As in other professions, the work done by a clergyman depends upon the man himself. It may be measured either by the way in which he discharges his duty, the number of duties he undertakes, or the character of the work to which he devotes himself. There is, however, no work which may be pared down so close as that of the minister of the Church. His commission is solemn and enormous, but the defined routine of his labours is practically small. When he lives a decent and sober life, performs the conventional services of his Church, reads a couple of sermons aloud on Sunday, and holds himself ready to advise and exhort the people committed to his care, 'as need shall require and occasion shall be given'—he being virtually the judge of such need and occasion—it would be difficult to bring him to book for any neglect of his duties. Compared with that of many in other callings, his fixed work is very light. It presents a remarkable contrast not only to that of the day-labourer, but to that of men in most liberal professions.

Practically the best part of his time is at his own disposal, and it is to the credit of the clergyman when, as is frequently the case, he is a busy or hardworking man. Though he is not paid for overtime, it is the exception to find him contented with the discharge of the bare duties of his post.

The question then arises, how shall he supplement these fixed functions, in what way shall he spend himself for the good of the people among whom he is placed? How shall he so use his position, opportunities, time, and strength, as best to serve God in the promotion of truth, righteousness, and love?

To some degree the form which his labours shall take has been conventionally determined for him. His weekday ministration, especially in the cities and towns of England, has somehow assumed a definite but often a small, monotonous, and depressing shape. He is frequently occupied in the discharge of minute fragmentary details which have come to be accepted as characteristic of his ministry; but the pressure of which sometimes, I fear, tends to dissipate or weaken his perception of the weightier matters of the law—the great law of

God, which rules the world. The importunity of small continuous demands upon his time and strength disposes him unconsciously to overlook or miss the operation of the great principles of life.

'Pastoral work,' as it is called, moves mostly in narrow ruts, and gives limited and broken views of the field of labour. House to house visitation, sick visiting, provident clubs, penny banks, institutes, day, night, and Sunday schools, classes, lectures, mothers' meetings—with the inevitable accompaniments to all these things of local regulations and petty discrepancies of practice—occupy his time. And yet, in the face of all this strenuous carefulness of industry, inspired by incessant desire to be doing good among the 'poor' or the 'working classes,' what is really their general attitude towards the Church as a centre and channel of Divine influence?

I refer mainly to that recognition of the minister's work which is to be seen in the attendance of those classes I have alluded to at the public services of the Church. This is, of course, not a final measure of righteousness, but it certainly is a fair test of the concern shown in the purely spiritual work or assumed spiritual work of the minister. And I fear that the most experienced will agree with me in saying that in cities, at least, this daily care and toil results in the smallest appreciation of the clergyman's spiritual mission by those for and amongst whom he mainly works. They value him chiefly for what they can get out of him in a worldly sense. I know that there are exceptions to this statement. Every clergyman can give examples of satisfactory religious appreciation of his weekday pastoral ministry. But, looking at the multitude of those amongst whom he works, these examples are not so much examples as exceptions. As a rule the bulk of them must be counted indifferent or suspiciously accessible. Let the parson grind ever so arduously in this semi-secular mill of pastoral routine, let him be provided with ever so much kind help in the way of district visiting and the like, and what is the result ? The poorest, most pauperised, and dependent among the working classes, look on the Church as a reservoir of tickets ; and the most independent shrink from, or civilly tolerate, any intercourse which professes to be religious, but which is quietly supposed or assumed to be tainted with a desire to patronise and dictate on the part of the parson and his church helpers. Thus his weekday work, especially in a crowded London parish, often comes to be small, monotonous, and depressing.

I am far from saying that I think these lesser ministrations should be despised or stopped. While people have bodies as well as souls, there must be care and kindness shown towards the physically helpless. It is impossible, however, for a clergyman to attempt the substantial and direct relief of the mass of 'those who want' within the limits of his cure. Other national agencies exist for this purpose. While he should be quick to perceive the necessities of those who by a judicious helping hand may be kept from slipping down into pauperism, his chief aim in that part of his work which is not directly clerical, but supplements his 'spiritual' duties, should be aimed at the *causes* of distress. A parson must not be above small ministrations, or affect unconcern for the least cares of the most commonplace life ; and every parish should be provided with pastoral machinery fitted to aid him in the exercise of true kindness towards the miserable and degraded; but there is an incalculably higher side to worldly ministrations than is exhibited in the constant effort to trim the ragged edge of pauperism and improvidence.

And even in the most judicious exercise of pastoral care for the needy, it is not the chief or conspicuous business of the parson to attend personally to these details. We have a very early example of the hinderance to the larger phases of ministerial work caused by the serving of tables, and the daily ministration to querulous widows. The first apostles soon found that these items of pastoral work hindered them in their proper business, which was chiefly 'the ministration of the Word.' And now the same little circle of minute importunity ever surrounds the man whose charge is, in the language of the Ordination Service, 'Take thou authority to preach the Word of God and to minister the Holy Sacraments in the congregation where thou shalt be lawfully appointed thereunto.'

Now I am sure that the parson of the parish is often perplexed and distressed in the consciousness of the pressure of duties not strictly in accordance with this charge. Many people, however, have small idea how much he is pressed with secular parochial personalities which have little or nothing to do with his real office. I must, therefore, for a little while, return to the picture, familiar to the eye of most parsons in London who serve in an anywise populous parish.

The same sort of people apply daily for letters to the dispensary or hospital, when in many cases all they want is a twopenny powder for the baby, or a pill to correct the disagreeable effects of too much gin. Every parish, too, has its share of floating semi-paupers who beg wherever they see a chance of netting a shilling or a ticket, and who are never radically bettered by the alms they manage to get. True, these alms occasionally serve to quench the hunger or warm the flesh of some poor body, and so shed a few rays of physical comfort on a miserable life, but they do not raise that life into a higher level. It is, however, very painful to adopt an attitude of constant resistance towards these dull suppliants, and to refer them to the relieving officer. It is, on the other hand, distressing to spend so much of year after year in blocking the weak balls which they bowl at the wicket of

'Charity.' It is also depressing to submit to their importunity, and, after having been thanked thousands of times, to find that part of the procession which is under your eye become perhaps a shade more importunate and shabby, while you are conscious that, as it disappears, another, I can hardly call it 'fresh,' squad is moving into notice, inheriting apparently the very clothes and difficulties of the first.

All this and such as this goes far to make what has in many instances (though with a deviation from the original purpose of his office) become the prescriptive daily work of the parson, sadly monotonous and disheartening. Especially is this the case in a commonplace town district, which is a fold without a fence, ever invaded on all sides by wanderers in the desert of London; and, after years of such toilsome application as I have just indicated, presents the same phases of improvidence and distress as challenge the enthusiasm of the new comer.

I cannot resist the growing conviction that far too much is made of these details. The parson must do some semi-secular work, but I am persuaded that it should be more organic and radical than it frequently is. If the minutely toilsome style of pastoral ministry which at present characterises the labour of a large proportion of the most devoted among the clergy is to be measured by its effect in attaching those on whom it is bestowed to the religious ministrations of the Church, it must, as I have already said, be pronounced a failure. If, on the other hand, this ministerial trouble of which I speak is taken merely with a view to relieve the most distressed among the poor of a parish, it resolves itself into an attempt to do what should be done by the law, and a parson becomes little better than an amateur relieving officer. The result in either case is the perversion of a sacred office and the promotion of a false feeble standard of clerical duty, or a waste of energy which might be better employed. The clergy, as a rule, are thus far too much exposed to the wearying service of tables. Many fret at and resent it with the distinct consciousness that the force and heat which should be reserved for their services and sermons, and for larger, more organic work, is frittered away. But they find it difficult, I will not say to shake themselves free from the accretions of accumulated parochial ivy which smother them, but even to loosen the clinging grasp which this system of petty secular ministration has got upon their order. I am sure, though, that in many a parish, especially in London, the oppressed and entangled parson would find an incalculable lift in his real work and genuine influence if he would draw freely upon his moral courage, and delegate to others many of these worldly ministerial details ; or, if he cannot find others to attend to them, simply leave them undone while he puts his back and heart into the work of his Church, into his services and sermons. These should come first.

I am the more forced to this conclusion by the aspect of that part of the metropolis in which I now live. The East of London is conspicuous for its preponderance of poor or working people. The perception that he is surrounded by thousands among whom he can hardly find a family or a person of leisure might compel the clergyman to shrink from any attempt to cope with the burden of toil he would bring on his shoulders if he set himself to minister individually to the detailed wants or importunity of everyone who might be likely to apply to him for some form of relief. He cannot, however, see distress, ignorance, improvidence, and dirt without the keenest pain. He must do his best to abate it. How shall he try to do so? My answer is, by allying himself with the larger forces of order and health; by working on radical organic principles, and not plaguing himself with the correction of the last ultimate details of the mischief that results from social imperfections. A parson is generally a man of liberal education, and capable of large views if he will use his eyes, and step outside the narrow field of vision traversed by a procession of semi-paupers, and spotted with little parochial sores. The minute experience necessarily gained in the sight of these should raise him from the letter to the spirit of ministration.

He is, moreover, frequently, in the East of London, one of the very few persons resident in his parish, who are in a sufficiently independent position to take a leading part in wide measures of sanitary and social improvement. Let him realise this, and not think to forward the real welfare of his district by only pottering after pauperized seekers of dole, and sitting at the receipt of halfpence and the distribution of tickets. He may do much more important and righteous secular work. Let him strive to promote any likely measure of social reform. Let him look for and use the wind of genuine public sentiment to fill his sails, and not make his back ache with paddling his canoe about the parish pond, and distressing his nostrils with the odours stirred up by every stroke of his oar. There is always some large wholesome scheme for the bettering of a district on hand, or capable of being set in movement. Let him turn to this. The parson should be in the forefront when a question about the cleansing, rebuilding, or sanitary bettering of any part of his parish is in doubt or under discussion. Let it be known, moreover, that he aids in this divinely, in the cause of righteousness. This helps to consecrate and strengthen the parochial influences that may be in operation. Few people, moreover, are so blind as not to see that this phase of clerical toil marks the exercise of a godly office. Thus his work cuts both ways. The message of the God of order is felt to be in utterance. The

truest and best friends of social improvement
respect the aid a parson thus gives, and see in him
a man who is not only 'kind' to the poor after a
small and fragmentary way, but who is an ally
and promoter of righteousness in the largest sense
of the word. And they hear with deeper confidence what he has to say in the more direct
professional discharge of his sacred office. They
look on him as a leading worker and colleague in
social reforms, and not as a mere kindly man
whose visits are always tinged with a suspicion
that he is about to ask alms in aiding some little
scheme for helping poor people, which generally
results in leaving them where they were, or perhaps
in encouraging the improvidence and beggary
which all deplore. Moreover, his strenuous pains
in promoting hearty services and good preaching
in his church will, as it gathers a sympathizing
congregation around him, chime in along with and
further these larger ways of work. Just as Christianity spread at first, by appeals to the centres of
intelligence and civilisation, the great cities of the
then world; so Christian work, closely allied to
' the ministration of the Word' in the congregation,

is forwarded by recourse to the wider organic movements of mankind, rather than by a minute, laborious, and persistent attempt to knit up the ragged fringe of distress caused in great measure by improvidence, and ignorance of the laws of life.

I am convinced, moreover, that devotion to small ways of work not only diverts energy from a much more effective way of working, but it weakens a man's power to 'minister the Word,' which is a leading phase of a clergyman's duty. I do not refer merely to the physical exhaustion inevitably attendant on prolonged pastoral visitation which, week after week, leaves a man to sit down to the Saturday preparation of his sermon with his boiler half empty of steam, but also to the sense of failure which accompanies a phase of parochial toil that does not result in bringing the poor to church, and to the small habit of thought which this is too likely to engender or confirm.

Perhaps my reader may think this is all very well, but what has it to do with the East and West of London? I reply, that though I, for one, cannot realise my ideal of what preaching should be, the´ necessity for pains in preaching has presented itself to me more than ever since I moved from the West to the East. In the West of London a clergyman frequently finds a relief from the irksomeness and depression of unappreciated week-day ministration among the poor, in the presence of a Sunday congregation mainly composed of educated well-dressed persons, who belong to a class which has inherited the habit of attending divine service, and who in some parts of the metropolis go to church as a duty, be the preacher never so dull and the service never so dreary.

I do not think it is so in the East. You could find, I take it, very few churches there which 'fill' as a matter of course. People as a rule don't attend service unless they are really interested. I do not say they do not come to 'worship ;' they certainly, however, are not indifferent to the sermon, and do not attend in any numbers where they are likely to hear a dull or lifeless one.

Of course, everywhere, an able and earnest preacher has a special 'following.' But I am persuaded that some men with no very marked natural gifts of preaching would find themselves well repaid in righteous influence and result, and lifted into interests which would sweeten and correct the depression of week-day toil, if they would devote very much more pains and time to the preparation or choice of their sermon than they do. Nay, I believe that, except perhaps in strictly pewed churches where the poor are virtually repelled by the arrangement of the fabric, they would find a grateful increase in the number of the working classes who attend the services of their church, if they would take more trouble about the 'ministration of the Word.' Working people in London do not attend public worship unless they are directly and distinctly interested in what they hear. It is not the custom of their class to do so, and thus the proper ministration of the Word to them is not solely a matter of divine impulses, but should involve carefully divine work. The putting of his freshest thoughts into the best language he can find, *i.e.* the best suited to his people, is part of the preacher's work. Let him jot down his hot thoughts, then let him hammer them—whether for 'extempore' delivery or not is not to the point; but he should cook his dish as well as he can, and not give it to the people raw. And when a man feels that he has a message to deliver, and takes pains to deliver it to the best of the ability that God giveth him, he is pretty certain to find some people of all classes willing to hear it. I am sure that if he worried himself less about the details of semi-secular ministration, or, by system, and by the getting of other people to attend more to them, shifted their continuous importunity from his mind, and used the time and force thus saved in the preparation of his sermon, *i.e.* in the ministration of the Word, he would anywhere work with larger aims, a better result, and more hopeful prospect.

I can fancy, however, that some might say, 'Oh, you really draw people to your church by mixing with them in their homes, and taking part in their social life.' I doubt if everyone can produce this result.

A man of kindly human heart, who in the daily intercourse of life is obviously ready to ' weep with those that weep, and rejoice with those that rejoice,' will naturally draw people by his ordinary conversation to attend the services of the church which he serves. He exercises the magic of charity, even though he does not bestow his goods to feed the poor. But the most conscientious and methodical system of ticket relief and tea-drinking entertainments does not lead them to church, unless, indeed, these doles and treats in the vestry or the schoolroom are made to depend upon their attendance in the house of God. In this case, however, the whole business of alms and worship is worse than useless. It degrades those who give and those who take.

The only legitimate 'attraction' to public worship—I use the word in its best, not in its histrionic sense—is to be found in the reverence with which the services are conducted, and the godly sense and warmth with which the Word is preached. Men are drawn to any good purpose only by devotion and truth, not by bribery. And this holds good whatever the sense may be to which the bribe appeals, or whatever the shape it presents.

THE general drift of this last chapter now leads me to remark, that I think the excessive entanglement of the clergy in minute semi-secular pastoral work, has been unwittingly promoted, to some extent, by the subdivision of large parishes in the poorest part of London. I would now, therefore, venture to say a word about this process, which has been adopted in order to meet what are termed the spiritual needs of large populations. In several places these subdivisions have been productive of much good. Some young broods dismissed from the parent nest have been able to take care of themselves. They have indeed not carried with them the vital spark of corporate life, but having within their boundaries a large admixture of classes, they have risen above sheer congregationalism, and become fresh centres of parochial vitality. In the case, however, of poor districts cut off from a mother parish, and having neither inside their limits, nor within easy reach, any reserve of well-to-do people, it has been found exceedingly difficult to rouse them to a feeling of corporate life, or even to retain such as the new district had originally contributed to the well-being of the mother parish. In these too often the 'new vicar' has been plunged, and left up to his shoulders in a pond of poverty. In some instances his individual enthusiasm and industry has floated the district during his incumbency, but it has sunk under other management. The 'poor' district parish gets no 'way' upon it, as a sailor would say. Its parochial life is intermittent, according to the energy of the incumbent. If he happens to be ill-suited, or to become exhausted, almost the whole parochial life stops.

This, of course, is in some measure true of any place or post, but it is sometimes specially and sadly conspicuous in the case of those which have no permanent parochial machinery that goes on working somehow, however deficient in energy and ability or fitness the incumbent may be. One of the thoughts that presents itself to me with recurring and special prominence, now that I am attached to the Mother Church of a large parish, though by no means a rich one, is the disadvantage under which some incumbents of what we call 'District Parishes' labour. I never before so appreciated the importance of the 'parochial unit' in ecclesiastical as well as civil life.

A 'District Parish' marks a departure from one principle of a national or established Church. It has no traditional corporate vitality. It inherits next to nothing of that which is historically associated with the idea of a parish, and which binds it together. Those secular affairs which are sometimes not sufficiently appreciated by the clergyman —though the connection of these with his post in a national Church is involved in the fact that the Rector or Vicar is generally the chairman of the vestry—and which secular affairs deeply affect the relationship between the people and the parish priest, are discharged by the vestry of the mother parish, in which body the distinctive existence of the district parish is unrepresented and unrecognised. Indeed, in most large parishes there are civil parts which do not coincide with its ecclesiastical districts. Along with the new portions cut off by the Ecclesiastical Commissioners are 'wards' or 'divisions' having no separate interests, but contributing to the convenience of central management. The ward or division has, however, no connection with the District Parish or its objects. That, for example, in which I worked for some fourteen years—I mean the district of St. Luke's, Berwick Street—though lying entirely within the parish of St. James's, Westminster, is not conterminous with the 'Berwick Street Division' of that parish. Its Incumbent and churchwardens, as such, have no place or voice in the body which administers its parochial law, and is responsible for sanitary and other regulations. If they take any part in any civil movement which concerns the ecclesiastical division of their parish, it is not an official part. The district churchwarden may happen to be a member of the vestry, but, as churchwarden, he is impotent and ignored. The incumbent fares worse, for though the old rector or vicar is generally *ex-officio* chairman of the vestry, and thus the interest of the clergyman in the civil government of a parish is recognised in the National Church, the new vicar can belong to the body which regulates the parochial concerns of the inhabitants of his district only by dropping his ecclesiastical claims and seeking election as a civil representative of ratepayers. It is true that in one way or another I myself, while at St. Luke's, Berwick Street, frequently interfered in questions which concerned the welfare of the mother parish, and involved that of the district ; and I many times spoke to the Vestry. I did not, however, belong to it. I had simply a voice by courtesy, but no vote, and no right to speak.

Moreover, in a District Parish even its peculiar socially religious business, such as that of baptisms and marriages, is frequently carried on with small reference to its separate existence. Almost all the marriages—*e.g.* from that of St. Luke's, Berwick Street—were celebrated at the mother church of St. James's. Though called 'a parish for ecclesiastical purposes,' it has often in the public mind no recognised corporate religious status. Being without those inherited social processes which compel the recognition of such an existence, and hold a parish together, it becomes practically a body without bones, a fold without a fence. To recur to my own experience, the residents, especially ratepayers, in St. Luke's knew very well that they lived in St. James's parish; but unless they were specially told so by the Incumbent or his assistants, they very seldom knew that St. Luke's was ecclesiastically the church of their parish; and when they were so told, they did not care two straws about the information. Indeed, repeatedly in the earlier part of my incumbency I was told by persons on whom I called, and who looked on me as a touter for local 'patronage,' that they preferred attending the services of their 'parish church,' *i.e.* not that of their ecclesiastical district.

My morning congregation was chiefly composed of outsiders, and though in time my evening congregation was fairly representative of the district, and was a good one, its members took no corporate interest in its existence. I state the following fact especially in support of what I have last stated. For fourteen years a meeting of residents in the district was summoned every Easter Monday to choose district churchwardens. And we never got a meeting. On each occasion we were obliged to send out to beg two or three neighbours to come in, so that the small quorum might be made which would enable us to discharge our business legally.

The flock of the district parson is, indeed, not so much a flock as a fortuitous concourse. His church work is mainly congregational, not parochial. Of course he differs from the congregationalist pure and simple in being the servant of anyone, let his religious persuasion or creed be what it may, who lives within the boundaries of his district. This is, indeed, the great practical use, the *raison d'être*, of the Establishment. There are frequently people who have occasion to use the services of a clergyman, but who are without, and have no desire to create, that claim upon his ministration which is involved in their being 'members' of his congregation or supporters of his schemes. Their wants are met by an Established Church. The parson is the minister of all within a fixed limit. Anyone living inside one of the divisions mapped and hedged by the Ecclesiastical Commissioners, after ignoring the parson for years, may summon him to discharge religious, ecclesiastical, and some social acts which legally require his concurrence. He has no right to refuse these ministrations to any within his bounds. He is a parish servant. But his public ministerial work generally takes a congregational shape; and in the District Parish this congrega-tionalism is inevitably most prominent; for there, as I have said, any corporate church life depends almost wholly on the personal influence and organising powers of the incumbent for the time being.

I was very much struck by this on coming to St. George's in the East, and comparing my re-ception by the residents in St. Luke's, fifteen years before, with that accorded me, a stranger, by the parishioners of St. George's. It is true that in time I made many kind friends at St. Luke's, but though I came with a good character from my last place in a neighbouring parish, the district, as such, did not care a button about the new man. It was otherwise at St. George's. There, on my first Sunday, a large number of representative parish-ioners attended the church simply because it was the parish church in which a fresh incumbency had begun; and a very considerable proportion of these were Nonconformists, who, though they had their own places of worship, and were strongly attached to them, entertained the parochial senti-ment so deeply as to leave them deliberately for that day, and give the new Rector a welcome. It was indeed distinctly intimated to me at the time that the concourse arose from inherited regard for the Parish Church, and that I could not expect to see the majority present themselves again. Now, considering that St. George's in the East has been made a bye-word of parochial reproach, and supposed, most unjustly I think, to exhibit an attitude of antagonism toward the Rector, as such, this reception of a stranger made a deep impression upon me. Numbers of Nonconformist parishioners went out of their way to greet him thus, simply because he represented a tradition which they respected, and a corporate sentiment which they felt. Here was, to me at least, a revelation of the strong life resident in the parochial body, and of the radical value of the parochial unit which is well-nigh lost or non-existent in a 'district.'

I must confess that this personal experience has, among other things, led me to question the wisdom of that continued subdivision of 'poor' London parishes which has lately been much in vogue. No doubt in all parts of the metropolis valuable zeal has been called into play under that

sense of personal responsibility which the district
Incumbent feels, and in the wealthier parts of
London these subdivisions have been followed by a
large increase in the work and the good done by
the Church. Such new districts having a fair admixture of classes within their limits, or near at
hand, have been able to hold their own, and in
many instances have become fresh centres of corporate life. But the mere abundance of population
in a parish is not, I think, a sufficient reason for
dividing it. In some cases the new district is not
only started without any tradition of distinct and
self-contained existence, but is from the first viewed
with the scant respect accorded to a 'poor relation.'
I believe that the good contemplated can sometimes be done without severance of relationship to
the parent stock, and at a very much less cost than
the creation of a new district parish involves. As
it is, great expense is incurred in the building of
new churches, which expense, moreover, involves
considerable permanent expenditure to keep up a
fixed consecrated building, when cheap mission-
rooms, officered by a well-paid staff, attached to
the Mother Church, would have done the needed

work as well or better. I will speak more of this presently. As it is, the help which might have been granted to the central work is sometimes drained or begged away for struggling districts whose Incumbents have to maintain a separate and costly 'plant,' and are always up to their ears in pauperism. Moreover, the sympathetic support and society likely to be enjoyed by a strong central body of clergy is lost in a partition of interests. I cannot help thinking that there has been enough of this carving of the old centres of parochial life in the poorer parts of London. You may cut slices off the original body, but you cannot inevitably propagate parishes, like verbenas, by cuttings. The new district is a new creation—in some places an excellent one; in others a new centre of despondency, in which the Incumbent has to fight an exceptionally sore battle, heavily weighted to begin with, and is cumbered with what is now an increasing care—the provision of assistant-curates who, as a rule, prefer the parish to the district church.

Of course it may be asked, What should be done in cases where the incumbent of a large mother parish is idle or incapable? Should not his incapacity be remedied by the introduction of fresh blood, and thousands of neglected souls be saved from the mischief resulting from central impotence? It must be remembered, however, that the character and capacity of a central Incumbent is necessarily uncertain. His ability is no more to be questioned or assumed than that of any Incumbent. An old populous parish may possibly, from illness, or accident, or other causes, be deprived for a time of suitable supervision, and during that time be so split up that a man of fair administrative powers, who could have organised the work of the whole place, finds himself positively hampered in his work by a partition of interests, in the creation of which large sums have been sunk. Possibly, too, in some cases, divisions of the original parish may be badly looked after. But they are 'parishes for ecclesiastical purposes,' and he cannot interfere; he cannot use the traditional corporate life of the mother parish with which he is associated, in remedying the deficiencies of the district.

I now feel that I have reached a patch of thin ice in my ecclesiastical course, and prepare to cross it with some apprehension. But it lies in my way, and it is not I who have made the path 'danger-ous.' I must get over it as well as I can, unless I shirk the spot, and devote myself to keeping in a safe and roundabout road. The point which I now wish to draw attention to is this. While considering the effects of parochial subdivision, we cannot avoid noticing that it is in district churches that the tendency some clergymen feel toward a development of their sacerdotal appetites has conspicuously grown, especially in London. I am here only observing a fact. I do not want to throw stones at Ritualists, for I hope I have sense enough to appreciate and rejoice at any good that may be done within the law. The true catholicity of a Church is measured, not by the number of those within its border who hold the same views, but by the varieties of opinion allowed to such as profess loyalty to its principles and doctrine. Still it must be conceded that they are chiefly district churches in which differences of opinion and practice have been pushed to an extreme; and it is there that they have struck such roots as they have. The Incumbent of a parish church is, however, necessarily associated with a body of laymen, who have it in their power to check excessive ritualism ; but in a District Parish the case is otherwise. There the Incumbent may generally do pretty much what he likes. It is mainly in district churches— I speak of the metropolis—that the confessional has been erected, that system of sacerdotal direction been revived, which, joined with a minute observance of ritual, has led to much disrespect for, and complaint against, the National Church on the part of the great body of laymen throughout the realm. These things are not tolerated in a parish which possesses a traditional governing body associated with the minister. I make no personal reflection on anyone. I appreciate and admire the ministerial devotion of many so-called Ritualists. All I want to do is to notice a fact ; and a fact is sometimes made clearer by an example.

My present parish, St. George's in the East, was once unhappily conspicuous for its riots ; but it must be remembered that the feeling out of which these riots grew was originally one of resentment towards what the bulk of the parishioners, rightly or wrongly, believed to be illegal sacerdotalism. Indeed, they were actuated originally by precisely the same sentiment as moved the House of Commons to pass the late Public Worship Act. It must be allowed, that though there were, no doubt, very disgraceful scenes witnessed under the roof of our church as the dispute grew, and though very many outsiders came from all parts of London to take one side or another in the strife, and though the strife was encumbered by the presence of some who cared nothing for the merits of the case, but came only because they liked disturbance, and wished to insult anything in the shape of religion, the original cause of complaint on the part of the parishioners was intelligible enough, and some form of resentment on their part defensible.

I must here pause to say that I do not think that these 'riots' were rightly apprehended. Each side naturally exaggerated that which was reprehensible in the conduct of the other. The scene was a curious one. Little thinking that I should ever become connected with the parish, I myself happened to be the clergyman who read prayers on the occasion of the police being first withdrawn from the church. When I came out of the vestry in the north corner to make my way to the reading-desk, I found not only every seat in the body and galleries of the building densely packed, but all the standing room filled. I had, at the risk of having my surplice dragged off my back, to work my way, shoulder first, to my place. Once there, I soon discovered that the pervading sentiment of the assembly was keenly theological. Almost all the congregation had prayer-books, and when the Psalms began, the effect was remarkable. There was a surpliced choir in the gallery which chanted, and some hundreds of sympathisers were present, furnished with Psalters, and chanting with them at the top of their lungs. But the bulk of the congregation preferred reading the Psalms, which they did in a sort of quarter-deck voice. The strain of human throat—the rush of sound—was tremendous.

Another phase of resentment I found to be associated with a certain red-edged book on the desk of the reader of the prayers. I think it was the hymn book. I know that when I took it up in my hand, and thus showed its scarlet rim, there was at once a deep inarticulate growl from all parts of the building. I remember that I several times tested the connection between this and the sight of the book; for when I lifted it up, apropos to nothing in the service, the growl came as surely as sound follows the laying of the hand on the keys of an organ in full wind.

I have referred to the ' riots ' at St. George's only as an illustration of my remark, that it is very difficult for a clergyman to introduce what the parishioners believe to be illegal ritual in a Parish Church. Even excessive ritualism, on the contrary, is frequently allowed to proceed without protest in District Churches. In these, or associated with these, there is no corporate body to originate or give distinctive weight to a protest, even though many or most of the inhabitants dislike the form of service used in their church. The residents in a ' district ' are as a heap of sand, without natural coherence. If they do combine, their combination presents the appearance of pointed sectarian opposition ; whereas, associated with a Parish Church, there is always a standing body of representative laymen wholesomely jealous of innovation, and whose protests are not necessarily connected with the spirit of factious criticism. I grant that many clergymen, especially those who are eager for what they believe to be improvement in the services, are likely to fret under this authoritative, or, at least, operative supervision ; and I have no doubt that real improvements are sometimes prevented by an undue amount of dogged local conservatism in old parochial vestries ; but the fact stands that in Parish Churches questionable innovations are not likely to be tolerated, and that those who dislike excessive ritualism have to thank the practice of subdividing the old centres of ecclesiastical life for the introduction of services which the bulk of laymen resent, if, at least, their opinions are exhibited in the voice of their representatives in the House of Commons.

There is another point worth noticing in the subdivision of large parishes in the poorer parts of London, and that is the temptation it offers to poor people to beg all round. One of the objects of the Charity Organization Society, now well known, is to prevent what is called overlapping in the application for and the distribution of alms. It is obvious that where there are several centres of distribution in one original parish, this mischievous overlapping is likely to prevail. I am sorry to say that poor souls in needy bodies sometimes do their best or worst to sell their adherence to this or that struggling congregation, or even small band of communicants. I have seen instances of this servile profession of piety again and again in different parts of London. The other day a poor man, with a wooden leg, stopped me in the street. He had originally been one of the communicants at St. George's, and I distinctly recollect his being one of the first to greet me when I came to the church with a great effusion of what, I thought, sounded like patronising compliment, and which seemed to say, 'You may count, if you conduct yourself aright, on my support.' He had left the district of the parish church when I afterwards met him in the street, and it was not my business to follow him, for I knew he had gone where he could be sure of careful clerical visitation. 'Reverend Sir,' he said, 'I know that I am not now living in your district, but as you are Rector, perhaps you may have the power of calling where you like. Now, I want to ask you whether you will visit me if I promise to attend your church.' He had prepared quite a little 'speech' with which he had loaded his piece. He had then carried it about at full cock ready to let fly when he should happen to get me within shot. I knew that he meant he would return to swell the number of our communicants if I would give him an occasional shilling, and of course I was obliged to disappoint him.   But his request betrayed a feeling which I know to be a common one, and is in divers places encouraged by the practice of avowedly giving the sacramental alms only to poor communicants.   Some months before I came to St. George's the former Rector had left, and the duty was done by a 'locum tenens.'   I ascertained that latterly during this interregnum not a single poor person came to the Holy Communion.   Directly I began my duties here a sad procession of them presented themselves at the altar rails, and early in the week made their appearance in the vestry to ask an alms.   Finding, however, that I did not confine our alms to communicants, they forsook the church.   Where they have gone I cannot say.   My old friend with the wooden leg was a sort of leader among them, and obviously wanted to make capital out of the fact that there was, as he conceived, a division of interests in the parish. The card he wanted to play was to get what he could out of the district parish as a resident, and net an extra coin or two by occasionally lending his countenance to us. Now, where a large poor parish is managed from a centre, with mission-rooms in various parts, there is no chance for the exercise of this commercial piety, which, I fear, is grievously prevalent in parishes where there is that partition of interests which must almost inevitably follow a splitting-up of a district originally attached to the Mother Church, into say a dozen district parishes, each of which has its own struggling charities and separate plant to support. Curiously enough, I have reason to believe that some local semi-paupers seldom beg of the clergy beyond the area of the mother parish. The congregationalism which I have alluded to as being specially characteristic of district churches, helps a clever pauper. He distributes his presence over as wide a religious field as he can, and with infamous catholicity appeals to the sympathies of several clergy, when if there were only one centre of charitable distribution in a parish his trade would be so far impossible. As I have said, it is a chief object of the Charity Organisation Society to prevent this overlapping, and to spot these piebald sheep. And its areas are in many cases conterminous with the original mother parishes. Thus it would appear that much of the evil which this Society has been created to remedy has been caused by the subdivisions of which I speak.

I must now venture on a word about one assumption in connexion with clerical work in London, which I think is in some degree fallacious. It does not indeed exclusively affect district parishes, though its acceptance has been one of the motives that have led those in authority to subdivide old parishes, especially such as had a large population of 'poor.' I refer to the assumption that if a man is incumbent of a parish with a population of only, say, 5,000, he is able to know the individuals who compose it, and so bring his flock under strictly personal pastoral influences. This assumption has been conspicuously operative in the action of the Bishop of London's Fund Committee. I desire to speak of that fund with the greatest respect, and I

wish it to be understood that my remarks apply
only to those large old parishes which contain the
chief 'masses' of the 'poor.' As I have distinctly
said, some subdivision, where the new swarm contains a large admixture of classes, has been found
to be eminently desirable and useful. But it is
otherwise with the section of an old parish which
is almost entirely inhabited by 'working people,'
and is made into a new parish for ecclesiastical
purposes, with a population of, say, 5,000. An incumbent is supposed to be able to know this to a
great extent individually, and so make them into a
'flock.' In the first place, this theory of a congregation attending a district church strictly from its
district will generally be found to be baseless when
looked at in the light of fact. I believe that most
incumbents will bear me out in what I say. I have
heard the statement uttered again and again, and I
might give many cases in which the congregation
of, especially, a district church is not composed of
those who live within the limits of the district assigned to it. I will, however, quote what I believe
to be a representative example. Some time before
I went to the district church of St. Luke's, Berwick

Street, it had an exceedingly popular incumbent. He gathered a large congregation. I have before me the list of those who took pews under his ministry, and their residences. Not above one-fifth lived within the limits of the district assigned to his church. It was much the same while I was there. People go where they please, and not where the Ecclesiastical Commissioners would send them. They attend churches where they like the clergyman or the service.

But to recur to the case I have mentioned—that of a district of 5,000 poor to which a new incumbent is appointed, and which has been cut off from an old parish in order to be brought under the influence of a pastor having the cure of their souls. I doubt if they are better looked after on the score of an additional minister being what is called an 'Incumbent.' He cannot really visit them himself. The question is not one of sentiment or ecclesiastical economy, but rule of three. It is decided by the inexorable authority of arithmetic. Taking the typical parish of 5,000 souls, or say, 1,000 families; and assuming that he has 250 days in the year available for house-to-house visitation,

the incumbent would have to make the acquaintance of four fresh households every day in order to
pay one visit only to each family in the course of
the twelve months. It would be discovered in
practice that, allowing for Sundays, vacations, and
other calls, nothing like 250 days would be found
in which he could sally forth with enough enthusiasm and time to put himself fairly *en rapport* with
four fresh households. Then think how difficult he
would soon find it to remember even the names
and faces and homes of those newly-visited sheep.
Take only six days' work of the kind I mean.
That would give twenty-four new families, wholly
unconnected with each other, whose acquaintance
would have to be made. What possible pastoral
influence could be exercised in respect to these on
the score of that visit, when every succeeding six
days of visitation added twenty-four more families
to the flock supposed to be thus brought under
individual supervision? It must be remembered,
too, that impressions, however deep and vivid,
could not be renewed or retouched till more than
twelve months had elapsed, during which time a
procession of strange faces and households would

have gone on obliterating the remembrance of those which had been seen weeks and months before. Moreover, the visitation I am supposing allows nothing for repeated visits to the same family, which, in the case of sickness, are necessarily made, and which in a population of some 5,000 would frequently occupy the whole of the time which a man could give to this kind of pastoral work.

A personal acquaintance with, and some measure of individual influence over, his flock is possible to a parson in some country parishes, for there the inter-relationship of the people helps him in getting to know them. Everybody is everybody's cousin. I judge by my own experience. Many years ago I had charge of a country parish of about 500 souls, represented by some eighty or one hundred households. There I certainly did know, and know something about, every man, woman, and child in the place. But, though I say it myself, this was done at the cost of really strenuous and repeated visitation. Now this population, centred in an old village, represents only one-tenth of a parish of 5,000 ; and I was very much aided in becoming acquainted with the individuals composing it by that inter-relationship to which I have alluded.

But in London the parson has little or none of such help. There the resident in the parlour by no means necessarily knows the lodger in the garret. Moreover, the poorer people in many metropolitan districts shift their lodgings continually, and are constantly flitting over the ecclesiastical border, while some from another district take their places. There the 'parish' becomes like a reach of a river, through which fresh fish are always swimming. Now if the incumbent, who is pressed with many duties peculiar to his position, tries to visit these systematically, he is overburdened, or he can visit them only by starving his other work. It comes to this, that, except in some possible cases of singularly exceptional and untiring energy, ability, and industry on his part, the notion that the incumbent with a cure of souls in a parish of 5,000 in London can by personal visitation exercise anything that deserves to be called pastoral supervision over his flock, is practically a delusion. He visits here and there as occasion arises, but he must look to other agents and agencies in order to 'work' his parish. He should indeed be captain on his own paddle-box, and know how the details of duty should be done; but he is compelled to do them by means of his staff.

And if he thus virtually delegates detailed and comprehensive individual work to his assistants, he might 'look after' a parish of 20,000 as easily as one of 5,000. Indeed, he might do it in some respects more easily. The same character of machinery would serve for either. He only wants more helpers—a larger crew. And a large ship is in several ways easier to command, more effective in warfare, and safer in storm, than a small one. But, if some theorists had their way, the ecclesiastical or parochial navy of the metropolis would be converted into a fleet of gun-boats—not invariably carrying guns.

I might also illustrate what I mean by an example from agricultural operations. A farm of 1,000 or 500 acres is not necessarily better tilled by breaking it up into a number of small holdings. On the contrary, the effect of the subdivision is to check the outlay of capital, and to lose the influence of organised and extended supervision. You get a number of struggling tenants who are unable to apply radical force of culture to the soil, and are yet individually encumbered and burdened with the expense and responsibilities of cramped independent command. So with the splitting up of some large 'poor' parishes into districts that are either too large or too small. They are too large for detailed personal visitation by the Incumbent, and they are too small for effective superintendence. In a parish of 20,000 or 30,000, however, you can have pastoral superintendence on a scale that admits of extended and organic work, that involves the use of corporate life and traditional powers. This may be effected by a very simple exercise of organisation. Let each visitor have either his own particular cases to look after—which, on the whole, is probably the best plan—or his district.

Anyhow every case is registered in one book. Every week the clergy and visitors meet and go through the list. A special advantage attached to this method is, moreover, the counsel which may be taken in difficulties. The whole staff takes some interest in each case, as it comes up at the weekly palaver. Each knows what is going on in the parish, and yet each has his district or set of cases, and probably his mission-room, where he forms his own congregation.   There is no overlapping either in the allotment of alms or in visitation.

All this power of central organisation is lost in the splitting up of the original condensed and crowded 'poor' parish into a number of districts, each of which has its Incumbent, burdened with the cares of incumbency and the expense of maintaining a separate Church Plant.

Another recommendation of this centralised system is the escape it gives from the difficulty now felt in getting assistant curates.   Far more lay-helpers could be used, and the clergy would be available for strictly clerical work.   Services in mission-rooms could sometimes be conducted by laymen.   Instead of there being half-a-dozen clergy in different churches to baptize each half-a-dozen children, or perform a single marriage per week, one clergyman would baptize fifty children and take a dozen marriages.   The people would come to the Parish Church for baptisms, churchings, marriages, &c.   The vestry of that central building would be open during certain hours daily for all ecclesiastical and religious inquiries, just as the civil Vestry Hall is open for all secular applications.

There would be one church thoroughly well worked, with plenty of services for such as chose to attend them on week-days, and security for immediate attendance in case any sudden need arose for religious ministrations, instead of half-a-dozen open for a short time during the day, or on two or three days in the week, perhaps at an inconvenient hour. I know, indeed, that some District Churches are seldom closed. But in truth, taking facts as they are, and as they are likely to be, it can hardly be expected that underpaid and undermanned District Churches should be constantly accessible, and kept going under a full head of steam.

The Parish Church, moreover, in the case I am contemplating, would be officered by a sufficient well-paid staff of clergy, amongst whom changes would not be seriously felt. But where there are half-a-dozen or more district parishes lying close round the Parish Church, each with, say, an Incumbent and a Curate, half the Incumbent's time is taken up with replacing his assistant, and much of his energy is spent in scraping together money with which to make up his stipend when he is got.

Now, except in the cases of widely separated or outlying districts, or where a large admixture of classes provides material for the abundant support of a new corporation, had the Ecclesiastical Commissioners, instead of creating new 'poor' parishes at very considerable expense, provided the old parochial centres with funds to pay assistant clergy liberally, I believe that the 'spiritual destitution' of the poorer parts of the metropolis would have been better provided for than it now is. These well-paid assistant clergy would have been provided with cheap mission-rooms, in which they would have formed and kept a 'following,' and where the services could have been conducted with greater freedom than is possible in a regular church; and they would have been aided by the sense of much individual responsibility, without being pressed by the cares which inevitably accompany the maintenance of a separate and costly establishment. They would not, moreover, have been exposed to that sense of isolation in their work which too often depresses the 'new vicar' of a parish almost wholly composed of poor, and who frequently cannot get a curate to help him.

Of course I am conscious that it is almost idle for me to write thus. The principle of the sub-division of poor crowded parishes has been, I fear, finally accepted, and has been widely adopted.

Churches have been built by the dozen which are more than half empty, and which are kept going, in many cases, only by repeated public appeals for assistance. Those who do attend them by no means live in the district which is assigned to the church. The clergyman is severed from the sympathy, and, I must add, inspection or control of those who represent traditional corporate life in the parochial unit, and the parochial system is, so far, virtually broken up. This, I fear, will have to be admitted as one result of the process which has been largely followed in the diocese of London. In the most thickly populated parts of the East, especially, the public would be surprised to learn how very thinly some comparatively new churches are attended—ay, and old ones too. Though, *e.g.*, we have on Sundays, in the evenings, a fair con-gregation in the body of the church at St. George's, the galleries are not filled, or anything like filled, except on some special occasions.

But, in divers cases, even where the Mother Church is scantily attended, a new district is formed, a man is sent to break ground there ; he gathers a congregation together in a room which holds perhaps from one hundred to one hundred and fifty persons.   Then comes the cry for a permanent church; but when he gets it, after distressing his soul with a period of importunate begging, the people who were willing enough to attend services in an unostentatious room are daunted by the primness and size of the new consecrated edifice; and the result is, in some cases, another permanent church with a vanished congregation.   Had small rough and ready licensed buildings been used, and the old ties with the traditional parochial sentiment been retained, I believe that more genuine work would have been done among the 'poor,' and money sunk in irremovable brick and mortar would have been saved for the liberal payment of missionary curates, who would, nevertheles, have not been cut off from the life that unquestionably survives in the old Parish Church, but which is weakened and impoverished by the partition of interests that inevitably accompanies the subdivision of a centre of parochial vitality. Had the old Parish Church been supplemented by mission-rooms, they might have acted as feeders from which some people might have passed on to the appreciation of the more formal services of the Church, while others might have preferred to worship ordinarily in a more homely fashion, using the Parish Church only for churchings, baptisms, and—as is now mostly the case—for marriages.

Moreover, provision might well have been made for communicants by increased number of celebrations of the Holy Communion at the central traditional church, at which celebrations the missionary curates could have officiated. Again, mission-rooms, not being consecrated, could, without any legal difficulty, be allowed to lapse into secular use in case a change in the character of the population, the displacement of buildings, or any other cause, should make such a lapse desirable. I must be allowed to repeat that the Parochial Economy which I have been considering in this chapter is applicable only to large populations of 'poor' resident around an old Parish Church, and not to those districts in the suburbs of London where a population containing a large element of church-going people could not be provided for by an old Parish Church, and where a new building is filled as soon as it is opened.

Bearing on the whole question which I have ventured to touch in this chapter is the far larger consideration that many other influences are now operative which were very weak when the 'people' were supposed to be tended in parochial folds by such as had cure of their souls. Then public teaching from the pulpit, and private sacerdotal direction really represented or involved the chief recognised means of popular guidance, and these were notably strengthened by some ecclesiastical discipline. The people were, moreover, in a great measure stationary and illiterate. But now the growth of cheap literature has provided a channel of information and instruction so wide and strong as to dwarf all commonplace clerical influences, and, eminently in towns, to dislocate the fabric of parochial economy. Moreover, such phases of ecclesiastical discipline as were once recognised and effective,

and traces of which still survive in some of the
rubrics in our Prayer Books, have practically died
out, and, except in the dreams of sacerdotal
enthusiasts, will never appear again.

The growth of public primary schools—supplemented, if not superseded, as this now is by
legislation involving a comprehensive scheme of
popular education—tends still further to depreciate
that mediæval machinery for the instruction and
guidance of the people which exhibits its chief
feature in the arrangement implied in the term
'cure of souls.' In cities people no longer attend
their parish church or consult their legal parson
except on purely personal grounds, or where
certain documents can be legally signed or certain
ceremonies legally performed only within prescribed
limits. 'Congregations' are formed quite irrespect-
ively of ecclesiastical demands or assumptions.
This makes the severe multiplication of fresh 'cures'
in cities somewhat questionable. The people are
already provided with that right in a parson's
ministrations which still survives as a useful feature
of the parochial system. Everyone is a parishioner
of some parish, and, if need should arise, can

command clerical services. But, as I have said, the very large majority of those in large towns who care for the public religious ministrations of the clergy choose their own minister, without any respect for ecclesiastical districts ; and if a parish is so large that one or two men are not enough to supply the demand for private spiritual ministrations within its limits, all that is wanted is only an increase in its staff, which is furnished at less cost than a new cure with its accompanying church, which is frequently doomed, in poor districts, to stand nearly empty.

CHURCH ENDOWMENTS.

THE foregoing considerations lead me on to say that, instead of adding to the number of churches in poor neighbourhoods, such as now exist might be made more effective by the abolition of some which have become practically useless, and the application of the money thus liberated to the provision of assistant curates in ill-endowed parishes. I do not plead for any considerable increase in the official income which the Incumbent has to spend, but for more money to pay for the work that should be done, and which money should be made payable to assistant curates, so that no greedy rector or vicar could pocket it himself. The unequal distribution, however, of such endowments as can support curates is prominent in the present parochial system. That system assumes that every parish shall be provided with sufficient parson power, and this assumption implies that means should exist to pay for it. But the official ways and means of the Establishment in the metropolis have now come to be unfairly applied. Lapse of time, change of population, and various other causes, have seriously disturbed the relation between clerical wage and work, which once, it is to be presumed, was fair enough.

There is, indeed, some recognition of this in the procedure of the Ecclesiastical Commissioners, and prominent witness is borne to it by Additional Curates and Pastoral Aid Societies; but the existing unfairness is so outrageous, that perhaps its very grotesqueness militates against its alleviation. If congregationalism were the law, we might expect stipends to be measured by the poverty or wealth of a congregation, but the parochial system means the provision of a parson in each parish. And where the population, and therefore labour, is or ought to be great, common sense indicates that the revenue of the individual church should bear a fair proportion to the duties which are or ought to be done in the parish to which it belongs.

But, in fact, this is not the case. Some large parishes, generally of the poorest, are left without adequate provision for the parson, who is responsible for their 'cure,' while others in London deserted by the parson in the week, and by the population on the Sunday, are excessively endowed. Their churches lie, dingy and silent, in the midst of a simmering world, like disused hulks anchored in the tideway of a busy river—paralysed witnesses to their original purpose, ghosts of parochial vitality—sepulchres of departed prayer, temples of consecrated vacuum.

Their priests frequently live away, perhaps in the pleasant places of the country, and on Sundays come up with two sermons in a little black bag, which they read to a sleepy beadle and a row of bare-elbowed charity girls, who look down from the gallery upon a congregation of solid and empty pews. This statement is rather exaggerated. Of course there is some one in church. I have before me a return, carefully compiled by an inquisitive but accurate friend, of his visit on Sunday mornings to fifteen of the City churches. He visited, indeed, a far larger number, and the congregation in the great majority was very thin. The fifteen I refer to were the worst attended. Still there was a congregation. In each case he scrupulously counted it. The result gave as the sum total of attendants in the whole of these fifteen churches only 291.

Among these worshippers my friend included every child that could walk, but he did not reckon officials or schools that were brought to church as a matter of course. The average number present in these fifteen churches was thus less than a score, all told ; and of adults probably little more than a dozen. But in either case the proportionate attendance of parishioners was possibly fair enough, for these parishes are almost empty of residents. Looking at the whole of the City proper, statistics give fifty-one parish churches to a population of about 27,000 within the walls. But this is taken from the census of 1871, and since then such changes and ejections have taken place that the total resident population of the 'City' is calculated to amount now to only about 20,000. And their use of the fifty-one churches which still stand in their midst is lessened by other considerations. The condition of their residence, in some cases, is that they should stay within doors, and thus many are unable to attend service if they would. The contrast between some of the rich City rectories, with this their scanty flock of human house-dogs, which keep Sunday watch over the locked-up safes, and the teeming perpetual curacies of the labouring suburbs, is absurd. It is as if a handful of wet sticks were lit to warm a draughty barn full of shivering souls, while a roaring furnace was kept up in an empty parlour. It must be remembered, moreover, that this crowd of fifty-one churches for 20,000 people does not include St. Paul's, which stands in their midst; and that there are other places of worship within the 'walls' of the City.

This conspicuous inequality is, I know, supposed by some to be mitigated by the consideration that there are so-called 'Prizes' in the Church. But this is a melancholy and degrading consideration. If it means anything it means that a poor parson, overwhelmed with undone work—for that makes the pressure of his burden—is supported by the hope that some day he may, possibly, get rich and easy promotion. But what becomes of the parish meanwhile? The provision of an adequate official income is for the place, not for the man. The parson is made for the parish, not the parish for the parson. Though the parson may be promoted, the parish is not. That is left in ecclesiastical indigence or 'spiritual destitution,' as it is called, and so the work remains undone. The tendency of the motive, moreover, is to lessen the poorly paid parson's interest in his duties, and to make an ill-endowed laborious cure of souls a mere possible stepping-stone to an easier or more lucrative office. I do not assert that this motive always or often operates. I believe, on the contrary, that the great bulk of clergy in poor parishes are devoted to their work, though in many cases they cannot get it done because they are not provided with sufficient funds to pay assistants. But the motive I have referred to is supposed to be operative ; it is supposed to mitigate the scandal of present inequalities. And all I can say is, that if it did generally operate, the richest and easiest offices in the Church would be filled by those who ought never to have borne sacred office at all ; and if it does not operate, it is idle to quote it as a consolation and support to those who suffer from present inequalities of endowment.

If the Incumbent of a poor parish involving laborious work were provided with funds to work it properly—and in such provision, I think the assistant curacies should be endowed, so that the Incumbent would be obliged to provide himself with a sufficient staff—it would be fair enough for him to look forward eventually to some easier cure, and hand over to younger arms the oar that he had pulled so long; but, as it is, the toilsome posts are in many cases comparatively unendowed, and those where there is least to be done are associated with the richest official incomes. Moreover, it is not even as if a lieutenant, charged with subordinate duties within his compass, received less pay, and might fairly look for promotion bringing more responsibility and stipend, but it is as if some colonels of the line received five times as much as others who commanded regiments demanding more special toil and expenditure in their management and supervision. It is as if, in the distribution of work over a farm, one field had £20 worth of labour spent upon it, while another, far larger and harder to work, had only £2 worth set apart for its share. It is as if the furnace of one engine that stood permanently on a siding were supplied with a ton of coals, while that of another that had to drag a train was stoked with a peck of cinders.

I do not think that the public realises the enormous inequality of the income of benefices in the metropolis. These fifty-one churches, for instance, still standing 'within the walls' of the ' City,' with its aggregate population of only some 20,000, have an average endowment about thrice as great as that of the Parish Church of Whitechapel with its resident population of 15,000. I have understated the contrast, for no accessible or easily accessible returns give the amount of these City endowments, since a ' parsonage ' there frequently means a house that the Incumbent lets for business purposes at a very high rent, while he lives elsewhere. Indeed, he really has no need to reside within the limits of his cure, and, of course, no blame whatever can be attributed to him personally. He does the duties of his post, such as they are, and it is no fault of his that he is excessively paid. Indeed, in many cases he chafes at the very small scope left for his enthusiasm and powers.

We want, however, a brave thorough readjustment of the glaring inequalities to which I have alluded. In the case of the City, if some forty churches were done away with as practically useless, and—all regard being had to existing interests—their incomes applied to the levelling up of ill-paid cures, and the provision of endowments for assistant curacies within them, very much of the inadequacy now set forth by Pastoral Aid Societies would be remedied. And if the sites of the suppressed churches, with their parsonages, were sold, it would be difficult to calculate the enormous sum that would be liberated to supply the deficient parson power of large and laborious parishes.

It would, without the exhibition of that gigantic importunity which is needed to scrape this fund together, go far towards providing as much as the Bishop of London's Fund ever tried to raise, and would do for the 'spiritual destitution' of the diocese what the Parochial Charities of the City could do towards the decent housing of the working classes of London.

It has been calculated that the Parochial Charities of the City could, without serious inconvenience to anyone, produce two million pounds; enough, according to an estimate of Sir Sydney Waterlow, to provide, if properly applied, sufficient sites for as many improved dwellings for working people as are needed in the metropolis.

RELIGIOUS OPINION.

WHILE I am committed to this rambling review of Church work and parochial economy, I am led to ask myself what kind of religious services seem to be most appreciated in the East of London, and I confess that I am perplexed what to say. The East of London is not a place which exhibits or requires a special ritual. Indeed, I fancy that, within reasonable limits, the form of service matters little, either there or anywhere else. People are generally most influenced in their estimate of the service by their own common sense or prejudice; and their attendance at any particular church is mostly determined by the character, sense, and energy of the individual minister. The habit of church-going is, however, not strongly marked in the bulk of those who live in these parts. There are comparatively few who attend public worship as a matter of course. We have no class which represents the unoccupied ladies who form the staple week-day congregations in some parts of London; and on Sundays, as I have noticed elsewhere, hardly any church in the East is filled as a matter of course. There is a marked respect felt for the old parish churches, though in divers of these the congregation is small; but the man generally determines the congregation, and supposing he has got something to say for himself, and says it heartily, I doubt whether the congrega- much care whether the service is what is called plain or choral.

The people like good congregational singing and hearty ministration; though, from what I hear, there is less appreciation of what is called advanced ritual among them than in some other parts of London.

As to the prevailing religious sentiment, I am inclined to think that while the people here are more individually critical and independent in their tastes than some I have been associated with, there is more distinct and thoughtful appreciation of what is generally understood by liberal theology in this than in other parts of the metropolis with which I am acquainted. We read and, I hope, think more than some would perhaps give us credit for. For instance, there is a lively Book-club among the leading parishioners, and thus the majority of the members of our vestry take in the monthlies, not excluding the ' Contemporary' and ' Fortnightly' Reviews. When I came to St. George's I was much struck by the interest which those connected with the parish church showed, not so much or so immediately in the form of service I proposed to have, as in the view I took of the great facts of religion. The first question I was asked in St. George's, in reference to my prospective interest in it as incumbent was, ' Are you acquainted with the Dean of Westminster?' On my replying in the affirmative, my questioner added, ' I hope some day you will get him to preach to us.' And when after a while I did so, and he was kind enough to come, the church, in the morning, was crowded to the utmost corners.

In respect to the form of our worship at St. George's, which, as many know, has been a ticklish subject here, I was impressed by the very little advice I received from residents. But I was con-

scious of being most keenly watched as to the line
I should take. Some two or three outsiders, however, who were anxious to see what people call a
ritualistic bent given to our services, pressed me
rather, till they found that I was hopelessly determined to follow my own judgment rather than
theirs. There are, I fancy, few clergymen who
have not been subject at one time or another to
external pressure in this direction, not so much
from *bonâ fide* members of their congregation, as
from volunteer advisers, who, with unattached
catholicity, look for openings in which to sow seed.
But I have found that these gentlemen, mostly
young, are far more desirous to make a parson
claim sacerdotal authority than to obey him when
he tries to exercise it over themselves. While I
was at St. Luke's, I was several times the subject
of an effort to bring on some development of ritual
in our worship. There is, I believe, a migratory
brotherhood, or confraternity, which takes as its
mission to go about and push ' Catholic usage,' as
it is called. I remember once we were invaded by
a gang of these devotees, who scattered themselves
here and there in the congregation, and by stu-

diously devout bowings and crossings tried to promote what they conceived to be improved gestures of reverence among the people. They gave us up, however, in about a month, and disappeared suddenly, like swallows.

I made very little change in the form and conduct of the services which I found here, except that, with the ready consent of the churchwardens, I relinquished such pew-rents as there were, and made the church wholly free. I also changed the hymn book, and introduced early celebrations of the Holy Communion, and Daily Service.

As for myself, I am of course well aware how interesting, even in an antiquarian point of view, all old usages become ; and that in ecclesiastical matters the question of vestments, attitudes, and gestures is by no means so trifling as some would make it out to be. It is nonsense to speak of ecclesiastical dress as a matter of mere church millinery, or even of æsthetic interest. The warmest and best instructed advocates of Eucharistic vestments do not care two straws about their intrinsic gracefulness or colour. The point is not the mere shape, texture, and tint, but the identification of the garments with those used in ancient Catholic days. The charm of the dress is not its beauty, or supposed beauty, but its significant antiquity. And those who oppose its revival do so thoughtlessly if they imagine that the mere attractions of colour and cut are desired. These could be secured while at the same time all that so-called Ritualists contend for was abandoned. Indeed there is radically nothing peculiar to any phase of doctrine in the making a church or service beautiful. It is a sentiment of religion that God illuminates His covenant with man in the colours of the rainbow.

The question, however, of ecclesiastical adornment does not, as I have said, now turn upon its mere splendour; and the ridicule frequently aimed at an insistence on such and such a gaudy sacerdotal garment is altogether wide of the mark. The thing in which those who strive for it are interested is to them as important as that represented by a flag. A flag is not a mere scrap of bunting tied to a stick or a pole. It is significant. It is not only used with especial prominence as a signal, but upon the lowering or raising of it the honour of a nation, or the issue of a battle, is made to depend.

Thus, too, when in the last sitting of Convocation a debate arose as to whether the word 'bread' in the Communion Service should be spelt with a 'b' or a 'B'—though one could not help thinking of the Bigendians and Littlendians immortalised by Gulliver—it was plain enough that deep matters were involved in this apparently trifling discussion.

Surely, however, we must all come to see that the great questions of the day lie beneath not only æsthetic arrangement but Catholic usage. They are incapable of being solved by the most devout and learned reference to the procedure of long ages past. New facts have come to light, new complications have arisen or been perceived, fresh methods of enquiry have been found ; and though extreme sacerdotalists do not deserve the sneers about church millinery which are cast at them, but rest their usage on a deep foundation, the time surely must come when they will look deeper still for the true grounds of faith, and the principles on which a matter which has ever interested men so much as the conduct of worship, should be decided.

Let us get back to St. George's and its ritual.

As the clergy of the Church of England are expected to wear some sort of ministerial garment
when they officiate, I use a surplice in the pulpit.
It is the handiest to put on, and involves no change
of dress during the service.

It is not, however, for me to talk much about
the mode in which our public worship is conducted.
I believe it is done 'decently and in order.' I may
say, however, that we have had a steady increase
in our Sunday congregation and offertories. Our
morning congregations, however, are what I call
decidedly thin, though in the evening, especially
during the winter, the body of the church is sometimes well filled, and a fair sprinkling of people
may be seen in the galleries. Some forty years
ago, or less, I am given to understand that it
was difficult to find room in the church on Sundays.
The conditions of the neighbourhood have been
wholly altered since then. The chief men of business connected with the parish resided within its
borders, and divers of them kept carriages and
livery servants. Now, a very large proportion of
our manufacturers and traders live elsewhere. Railways, steamboats, and trams have created a resi-

dential revolution.   One result of this has appeared in the gradual thinning of the congregation of the Parish Church.   Indeed I have been told that now it is hopeless to think of filling it again.   It has, people say, been deserted too long.

However, the chief object of the parson is not to 'fill' his church.   He can but do his best, and preach according to the proportion of his faith, avoiding at the same time anything like a request on his part that such and such persons should 'come to hear him.'   When I have found a man attending no place of worship at all, I have sometimes advised him to use this neglected phase of life and interest ; but I have never asked anyone to attend my church.

In respect to those who choose to come, I am glad to say that the congregation joins very heartily in the services, and is as intelligently attentive to the sermon as any I ever preached to.   The number of our communicants has also grown.   They are very few in proportion to our population, but their number increases.   Last Easter Day we had about 100.   In our ministrations we are happily much helped by the fact that the acoustic pro-

perties of the church are excellent. Every syllable
is perfectly heard from the desk, communion table,
and pulpit.

The church is a solid roomy structure of the
Wren type, built by Hawksmoor and Gibbs some
150 years ago ; and its proper name, according to
parish archives, is ‘St. George, Middlesex.’ Its
internal lines strike me as being remarkably good,
and it is capable of much genuine decoration in the
way of colour, and especially of mosaic. The fittings
of the church are of oak, and the pulpit is a roomy
imposing fabric, which they say originally cost
some £700. It is elaborately carved and inlaid,
and is made of the same wood as the seats. The
building itself is constructed of Portland stone, and
has a tremendous tower, which shows far above the
line of roofs, when the atmosphere is clear enough,
to a spectator on London Bridge. Indeed I am
told that its height is within a few feet, one way or
the other, the same as that of the Monument ; and
I can well believe it, for the view from its summit
is remarkably extensive. Looking down on the
red brick rectory from this altitude, my house,
though three stories high, shows like a brown box

in the churchyard, and the tombstones seem no bigger than dominoes. From the summit of our tower we fly a huge flag on all suitable occasions ; and I must pause to notice a singular accident which befel it one day last summer. A great storm had come on, with thunder and lightning. I happened to be away for a few hours, and on my return only half the flag was flying from our staff. It had been severed by or in a flash of lightning. Several persons saw the outer half of the flag cut clean off from the rest and flutter down into the churchyard in the middle of a great flash. Sure enough there was one half on the ground and the other still flying ; and the division seemed to have been made as accurately as if it had been rent in twain by an invisible hand. This was in Whitsun week.

But I must descend, and mix once more in the living world below. Though I have been always fortunate in my lay as well as clerical colleagues, I could hardly have expected to find churchwardens more interested in the work of the church and conduct of the service than those I have hitherto been associated with here. They are both appointed

by the vestry, the rector's right to nominate one
having somehow lapsed. In the first year and a
half of my incumbency they collected and spent
£400 in the internal equipment of the church,
without my asking a single parishioner for a penny.
This, however, was a strain upon our resources,
and there is much more to be done. For instance,
our organ, the relics of which are concealed by an
imposing case in the west gallery, is pronounced
to be hopelessly beyond repair. We do not use it,
but lead the choir with a small instrument which
is placed in the chancel, and which we are obliged
to hire.

As to local sentiment and life, it strikes me
that here in the East the people are eminently
freespoken and keen to criticise. I have noticed
on their part a shrewd sense of humour and a
quickness to resent any imperious pretensions. A
thoughtful friend, who knows this part of the
metropolis well, once said to me, 'The East of
London is the place to learn courtesy.' I hope I
may not miss the value of his suggestion by any
rude or clumsy comments of my own upon it. He
does not mean that we find here any strongly

marked relics of feudal obeisance. These are
chiefly to be discovered in the still nooks of the
country, where the old order gives place but slowly
to the new. And as a yet living inheritance from
the strong past these relics are not to be sneered
at ; and he is no true philosopher or reformer who
would hastily laugh them down or stamp them out.
But other conditions and shapes of life have arisen
in places where the directly dependent relation
between different classes of society has become
obliterated or been much watered down. In cities
especially this is sometimes succeeded by an
attitude or expression of bumptious independence
on the part of those who form what are called the
working classes. A man, however, who has a
healthy perception of human life will see that
there can really be no individual independence in
a civilised community. We are every one members
one of another. But the outward expression of
marked respect comes to be reserved for those who
are felt to deserve it. Here the people are civil
enough when accosted civilly by a well dressed
stranger, but there is no touching of hats to goodly
apparel and a gold ring. The original ground

upon which they go—the principle assumed by Easterners, whether Liberals or Conservatives—is equality. This is an excellent place for a man to find his level in. If he is really respected, respect is shown freely to him, but if he gives himself airs he is made aware of his mistake. I cannot quote instances, but I have somehow felt that any pomposity on the part of a local public man here would soon make itself unpleasantly felt by him.

This recoil of imperiousness is much more likely to be felt here than in the West of London. There a man may, perhaps unwittingly, give offence by his manner or what not at a local gathering or parochial celebration; but unless some Christian friend rebukes him to his face, or takes the trouble to inform him by letter of the bad impression he has created, it is possible that the offender knows nothing of the matter. But, even supposing that he is thus rebuked, in the first case few beyond those present at the meeting know anything of the remonstrance; and in the latter, even though he makes some wholesome resolve in the way of improvement, the censuring epistle goes silently into his waste basket. Here, however, machinery exists for immediate public reprisals in the shape of a local press, which none are too big to be hit by.

We have, indeed, a large circulation of the leading London penny journals—the *Standard, Daily News,* and *Daily Telegraph.* The *Times* is little read. We file it at the Vestry, but it is too dear for local use. I take it in, but unless I ordered it I could not get a copy at any of our newspaper shops. I fancied, however, that I had found a neighbour with a special literary or political interest in the leading journal. My copy of the *Times* goes on the second day to a worthy butcher hard by, to whom it thus comes cheap. On one or two occasions, however, when I wanted to refer to something in the copy of the previous day, and sent to beg the loan of it, I found that it had been torn up. The truth gradually revealed itself to me that my practical neighbour preferred the *Times* because of the toughness of its paper. He desires to have the news, but is content to get it rather late if printed on material tenacious enough to hold small parcels of meat without bursting.

But we read the leading penny dailies extensively.

Beside these, however, there are several local papers conducted with considerable ability, and read by all. These keep a sharp eye on everything that goes on, and no local public man can make a slip without its being known by each one of his neighbours. In the West of London there are no such generally recognised inspectors of social and parochial life. Most people there take in only the large London journals, and a parochial event must be of exceptional magnitude to find its way into them. While, *e.g.*, I was working in St. James's, Westminster, I caught no steady echoes from any local publication; and on taxing my memory, though I believe that there was some parish organ, I cannot tell its name, and cannot recall any influence it exercised. Here we have at least three or four weekly papers, either of which is a looking-glass, giving reflections of every local event or gathering in the least out of the ordinary parochial routine, and chronicling the speeches at all the fixed parochial parliaments. And these are generally read by all the residents in the parish. None are too great or too grand to feel or profess no interest in them. Moreover, sermons, lectures, &c. form a very frequent feature of their contents.   They are obviously much used by the clergy, ministers, and congregations of churches and chapels.   Some months ago, *e.g.*, there was a prolonged controversy on the Catechism between several prominent clergymen and Nonconformist ministers carried on in their columns. Such public strife would, I am inclined to suspect, be almost impossible in the West of London.   The large papers would not record it; and if any others did, the chances are that few in the congregations of leading West End clergy would know anything at all about the business.   Here, however, week after week, in the *East London Observer*, the *Eastern Post*, and the *Tower Hamlets Independent*— besides, I have no doubt, other papers which I do not happen to take in, but which represent important local influence—the 'Catechism controversy' held a prominent place, and was read, or at least was printed, with the expectation that it would interest and be read by, all.   And very sharp it was while it lasted.   There is now, too, while I write, a public debate concerning the truths of Christianity going on between Mr. Bradlaugh and a minister, and the blows of the two battledores are heard in our local press. I, for one, regret the making of a creed into a shuttlecock, and the tempting of the public to suppose that real good can be got out of a game like this. But anything in the shape of a contest is always interesting. However, my illustration is too tame; this is a fight, not play, and as here the combatants mean fighting, and have no tips to their foils, I suppose that some especially care to see which of the two will in their estimation get the best of it. Happily the poor creed is in such encounters least thought of, the concern of the spectators being chiefly to see who can hit hardest or stab deepest. These conflicts on presumably great truths soon pass into personal strife, even though both sides may manage to avoid personalities. The most decorous people have no objection to see their man slay his opponent, provided he will do it politely.

While, moreover, these popular local organs render it impossible for anything to be done in a corner, and visit an offence or presumed offence upon the head of the offender at once, they provide an eminently useful channel for announcements, and the utterance of opinions which, elsewhere in

London, or at least in the Western portion of it, a clergyman could not well convey to the bulk of his parishioners without the very expensive process of printing a pamphlet and circulating it amongst them. Here, by the courtesy of their editors, I, like others, can generally speak through them to the whole of the parish; and if anyone wants to criticise myself, he finds no difficulty in doing so with complete local publicity. Indeed, in this respect, East London resembles a provincial town. These papers thus provide means for a very fair test of Eastern public opinion about the conduct of the services in the various churches and chapels, and I seem to know in a couple of years very much more about my clerical brethren and their ways than I could have known in a lifetime while in St. James's, Westminster. We all see and hear one another. And it strikes me that if there is anything which the Easterners are sure to resent it is what I might term dictatorial sacerdotalism on the part of a clergyman. They don't seem to have any marked objection to such features in the service as surpliced choirs, &c.; and in those cases of 'advanced ritual' which do not mean mere show, but sincere and loving work, I do not recal any unkind comments. The intention of the business is recognised as good. But let a man give himself airs, let him exhibit any of the excommunicating spirit, and then the public—represented by both the Liberal and Conservative local press—is down upon him with a vengeance.

As an instance, moreover, of the free and independent spirit in which religious questions and practices are sometimes approached here, I might quote the coolness with which the services of Messrs. Moody and Sankey were dissected by our local press. These revivalists came with amazing reports of their popularity and success in the North of London; and then, after a week or two of inquiry and inspection, the ‘East London Observer,’ which has the character of being our most widely circulated paper, sat upon them with supreme disregard of the accumulated laudations they had received, and proceeded quietly to dissect the whole movement; approving of some things, but disapproving of much that went on at the Bow Road Hall, and the influence it was likely, in the writer's mind, to have upon the interests and progress of sound religion.

Much as I thought I knew of the independence of our local press, I confess that I was surprised, in the full metropolitan blaze of the revivalists' popularity, and while some of the large London journals seemed puzzled what to say, to read in a local paper, widely read among those who were most likely to be attending the services in question, criticisms on the movement, written as coolly and philosophically as if the scene of the revival lay at Chicago itself.

PERHAPS this would be the place in which to say a
word about the help which some laymen resident
in the West have been kind enough to give in the
pastoral and social work of the East. I cannot help
thinking that this matter has been much misunder-
stood. An impression has somehow got abroad that
the East is in so degraded and miserable a condition, that a man of means and leisure who devotes
some of his spare time to visitation among those
who reside in it, is a sort of missionary martyr;
but that, if he can bring himself to penetrate the
dim regions beyond the City, his mere presence
there will be sure to shed sweetness and light.
Now I believe that any man anywhere, who in all
truth, humility, and godliness seeks to do good,
will see of the travail of his soul. The assumption,
however, that the East of the metropolis is really
worse in a moral sense than the West, is one that

needs the testimony of fact. It is true that here, as a rule, there are more poor in proportion to the rich than in the West, and I am sure that we should be benefited by a better resident mixture of classes. There is, I fear, not much chance of this, since a sort of centrifugal force, which is in operation over the whole of London, is ever sending the most successful among its traders and manufacturers away from the scene of their daily business to reside in or near to the country. As it is, we residents in St. George's are almost all of us obliged to work for our bread. We have no gilded youth, we have few idlers. But I have yet to learn that a region is necessarily degraded because it has no opera house, polo clubs, or footmen in powder. Indeed, at the risk of being considered an ungracious heretic, I am inclined to think that if it comes to a question of teaching and example, the West has quite as much to learn from the East as the East from the West. The East is distinguished by a steady and laborious discharge of duty, which before God is of great price. It seems to me that the West does not apprehend the force that may yet be latent in a famous sentence once uttered concerning the interest of the poor in the Kingdom of Heaven, and which can hardly be obliterated by any exhibition of the small enjoyment they feel in the services of those various chapels and churches which are half empty in these parts. Goodness may not be altogether measured by attendance at public worship. And 'our betters,' to whom we should order ourselves lowly and reverently, are by no means necessarily to be recognised by the clothes they wear, or the nicety of the food they eat. I grant that a larger proportion of families among us, not pressed with the necessities of toil, would have a wholesome influence. They might make themselves useful in many ways connected with the local advancement of desirable social and civil measures; and the resident attached presence of more men of ability and leisure would help in breaking the dead level of labour, and bring fresh blood into our veins; but I think that people in general hardly realise the sterling industry and independence of the present East of London. It is not a colony or concourse of Lazaruses, sitting distantly at Prince's Gate, and desiring to be fed with crumbs of comfort from Pall Mall. The poor in the parish of St. George's in the East certainly 'beg' much less than in that of St. George's, Hanover Square, or St. James's, Westminster. I was once curate at St. Mark's, North Audley Street, for five years, and know that what I say is true. As to St. James's, Westminster, when I first went to St. Luke's I frequently found some forty or fifty applicants for alms at our daily session in the vestry ; but here, to my surprise, when I came, and therefore might have been supposed to represent a possible fresh store of tickets and shillings, comparatively very few beggars made their appearance, though some of the regular 'poor' communicants soon presented themselves to ask an alms. But as for such sheer begging as I knew in the two great Western parishes I have referred to, all I can say is, that we have nothing like it in this part of the East. I have frequently known a week pass without a single application for alms at our vestry. The Eastern poor are more virtuously independent than the Western. Moreover—barring the laxity of crews on shore, and their dissolute parasites, of which I must say something more presently—there seems to me less drunkenness in our streets than I saw in those of Soho. We have, it is true, much grievous intemperance, but I fail to see, *e.g.*, as I did in the West, those groups of tipsy tailors, who represented much of the resident work of the place; but, especially on Monday mornings, might be observed lounging at most corners of the street. The working classes, on the whole, are an independent, industrious race in these parts of London. Now, if a gentleman who has contracted the habit of associating toil with degradation comes amidst our workers with a full pocket and a soft heart, he is likely to do more harm than good. You can hardly expect poor people to have virtue enough to refuse unexpected doles. Anywhere, I fancy, a smiling lavish donation of money would buy blessings and thanks by the bushel. But a man who thus purchases these must not think, as he drives home Westward, that he has really benefited the people amongst whom he has made a descent. I have reason to believe that some districts have been seriously pauperised, and thus injured, by means of the Western money that has been thus given away in them.

It might be asked, then, what would you have

those do who reside in the wealthy parts of London, but are honestly desirous of helping such as inhabit the region of strenuous labour that lies East of the City? There is a scope for the exercise of their kindliness and the outlay of their money, without pauperising those whom they would aid. Let them, *e.g.*, come and help, in a kindly way, in concert with those who know most of the place and people, and who are trying to benefit them organically. If they are able and inclined to relieve cases of individual distress, let them do so in co-operation with the local Charity Organisation Society.

Or let a man do a defined Christian work, gathering together and periodically teaching and counselling a class of lads. Let a lady make friends with a class of girls, or undertake the kindly visitation of certain chronic sick. There are many ways in which a person of leisure and perseverance, living in some other part of London, could do a distinctly good work in the East. But a mere gadding about of a Lady Bountiful, with halfcrowns, would do much more harm than good. Any work, moreover, here—as well as elsewhere, to be of use—must be punctual, sustained, and done in a spirit of respect for and civility towards those whom it is intended to benefit.

If would-be helpers of the East wish to work on a larger scale, they may, *e.g.*, promote the erection of new dwellings. It is obvious that these are more easily provided where sites are cheap, and such dwellings are not only appreciated, but pay the promoters a fair interest. We have much room for improvement in respect to houses for the working classes, and the price of land, which checks these operations Westward, is not a hindrance here. Let those who would benefit us also help in the provision of such institutions as baths and washhouses. Let them aid in the establishment and conduct of Penny Banks, or anything which tends to make people help themselves, but let them not think to aid us by opening out fresh ponds for beggars to fish in. Let them not peril or impair that sturdy independence, which is, as I think by comparison of it with the West, one of the striking features in the East. We want, moreover, some phases of decoration, some touches of beauty and refinement, for the promotion of which we have small leisure and little money.

But I must not pursue, in this chapter, the consideration of several matters which belong more fitly to our review of the physical and social aspects of the East of London; or might suggest themselves when I come to say a word about some of the various trials, hopes, and prospects which it has been my lot to make or entertain in working either in the West or East.

I SUPPOSE there is no part of London without its special trade or manufacture. Some callings, associated with constant immediate and universal demand—such as those of the baker, butcher, and publican—are, of course, spread evenly over the whole of the metropolis. Daily bread, meat and drink, must be easily accessible. But with the exception of bread, I am (for the moment) at a loss to think of anything in large and constant use which is not produced at special centres of industry, and then widely dispersed. This dispersal from the centres is continuous and conspicuous. But your baker is generally local, he goes mostly on foot; or if he has two wheels, drags his own load, and produces behind his shop the commodity which he sells. Meanwhile his neighbours—the butchers, grocers, linendrapers, and publicans of his district— bring their goods from a distance. With some partial exceptions the articles in commonest demand are manufactured wholesale, and then distributed to be retailed.

It would, however, be difficult to determine the causes of the selection of various parts of London for the production or storage of some articles of commerce. There is historical cause for the presence of silk-weavers in Bethnal Green and Spitalfields. Possibly there may be some equally good reason for the prevalence of watchmakers in Clerkenwell. The chemical manufactories at Bow were placed there I suppose, originally, to be beyond the range of the metropolitan nose. The crowd of minutely precise trades, such as those of dressing-case makers, hand bookbinders, engravers, &c. &c., located in Soho, are probably drawn there by the high pressure of the demand for the immediate supply of artificial wants which characterises the region of shops that minister to condensed and luxurious civilisation. Soho exhibits the fringe of skilled high class manual workers which has floated up from the centre and East of London towards the long-pursed territory of the West. The neighbourhood of the River and the Docks displays the paraphernalia of the sea and shore. Slops and sextants, deck-boots and telescopes, are offered in what, to an outsider, appears a superfluous abundance along the bank of the Thames east of the Tower. There, too, may be found rope-walks and sail-lofts. Many of the manufactures and trades associated with seafaring life are carried on in our part of the city. They are indeed common to all seaports; but of these London is the largest, and thus they abound among us.

In or near to St. George's, however, we provide things for which there is the widest and narrowest market. If anyone were to ask me what were the two articles most characteristic of the commerce of this neighbourhood, I should say sugar and wild beasts. We are, or rather were, conspicuous for our bakeries of sugar; and we hope we shall be again. Out of some five-and-twenty in the whole of London and its suburbs, you might count the chimneys of more than two-thirds from the tower of our church; and the factory which produces the best English loaf sugar stands within a few hundred yards of the church gate. The raw material is landed hard by, in a shape unattractive to any but flies and greedy little boys, who cannot keep their hands from picking at anything sweet however coarse, and, especially after school hours, buzz round any sugary waggon in which there is a leaky parcel.

Hereabouts we have transformed the coarsest brown stuff into loaf sugar. But this trade is now very much depressed. Indeed, there are some who think it wellnigh destroyed. I am informed that in 1864 there were twenty-three producers of loaf sugar in London. Since then their trade has shrunk very seriously. A short time ago I believe only three survived, and the chief of them, in St. George's in the East, has ceased operations in the course of this year. The action of the French Government in encouraging, chiefly by a bonus, the exportation of home made sugar, has, at present, made it impossible for the British manufacturers to compete with the French. But as this advantage is given to a special branch of industry in France by the taxing of its whole nation, it is to be hoped that French eyes will be opened to the matter, and that the cloud will pass away from the British trade. Especially is this desired at St.

George's in the East, for, as I have said, sugar refining is, perhaps, the most ' conspicuous ' trade of these parts. I have thus let my reference to it stand uncorrected, though at present our furnaces are cold.

In respect to the other article to which I have referred as characteristic of the trade of St. George's, and which may be considered peculiar to it, I suppose that there is no other place in the world where a domesticated parson could ring his bell and send his servant round the corner to buy a lion. Had I a domestic capable of discharging such an errand, and a proper receptacle in which to put the article when brought home, I could indulge the whim for a lion at five minutes' notice. My near neighbour, Mr. Jamrach, always keeps a stock of wild beasts on hand. Anyhow, if he happened to be out of lions, I should be sure of getting a wild beast of some sort at his store. A little time ago one of our clergy, who knows of almost everything going on in the parish, happened to remark to me that Mr. Jamrach's stock was low. He had just looked in, and the proprietor said he had nothing particularly fresh then, only four young elephants and a camelopard, beside the usual supply of monkeys, parrots, and such small deer.

The wild beasts are kept in Betts Street, within a bow shot of my door, but the shop in Ratcliff Highway is always full of parrots and other birds. The attitudes and gestures of those exposed for sale are always curious and sometimes comical. I was much struck the other day with the pose and expression of a posse of owls on view. They sat side by side full of thoughtful silent wisdom, with just a twinkle of possible humour in their eyes, like judges *in banco*; while in an oblong recess within the shop beyond them there were twenty-four large and perfectly white cockatoos standing in two precise rows, shoulder to shoulder, and giving out their best notes, exactly like a surpliced choir. In another room were two thousand parroquets flying loosely about, or clustering like flies upon the window frames in ineffectual attempts to get out. The incessant flutter of this multitude of captives filled the air of the apartment so thickly with tiny floating feathers that they settled on our coats like flakes of snow. We came out powdered. The twitter in the room was, of course, incessant and importunate. There is a great demand for talking parrots. Mr. Jamrach always has orders in his books for more than he can supply. The parrots kept in stock are all young and unlearned. They look like the rest, but education marks the difference in the world of birds as in that of men. The selling value of wild beasts varies very much. You must pay about £200 for a royal tiger, and £300 for an elephant, while I am informed you may possibly buy a lion for £70, and a lioness for less. But a first-rate lion sometimes runs to a high figure, say even £300. Ourang-outangs come to £20 each, but Barbary apes range from £3 to £4 apiece. Mr. Jamrach, however, keeps no priced catalogue of animals, but will supply a written list of their cost if needed. He does not, moreover, 'advertise,' so much as royally 'announce' his arrivals. Certain papers in London, Paris, Berlin, and Vienna, occasionally contain a bare statement that such and such beasts and birds are at 'Jamrach's,' no address being given. He has customers in all the Zoological Museums in Europe, and the Sultan has been one of the largest buyers of his tigers and parrots.

Once, some long time ago, a disastrous and

distressing accident happened in connection with this store of wild beasts. One of the tigers in transit escaped from his cage in the neighbourhood of the Commercial Road. Finding himself free, he picked up a little boy and walked off with him, intending probably, when he found a convenient retreat, to eat him. Of course, the spectacle of a tiger walking quietly along with a little boy in his mouth (he had him only by the collar) attracted the notice of residents and wayfarers. Presently the bravest spectator, armed with a crowbar, approached the tiger, and striking vehemently and blindly at him, missed the beast and killed the boy. The tiger was then secured.

Mr. Jamrach has great and, I suppose one might say, mystic power with beasts. His business, though, is not confined to the animals of the earth and the air. You may find curious products of the water in Mr. Jamrach's back-room. I especially recollect a vessel of telescope fish from Shanghai, queer little creatures with eyes starting out of their heads like the horns of a snail. These were on their way to the Brighton Aquarium.

Besides the store of birds, beasts, and fishes, there is a collection of all sorts of heterogeneous things from all parts of the world—armour, china, inlaid furniture, shells, idols, implements of savage warfare, and what not. Mr. Jamrach not only collects in comparative detail, but does not overlook the promising purchase of a whole museum. Some time ago he brought one in the lump from Paris. No wonder that the Ratcliff Highway is visited by many with money in their pockets for the purchase of antiquities and curiosities. From what I have seen I fancy that sometimes a good judge of these things can pick up a bargain here.

Beside that of Mr. Jamrach's, we have divers shops for the sale of birds, especially parrots, and I imagine that many a sailor turns his collection of foreign curiosities into money within the limits of St. George's.

Of course, one main feature of the catholicity which I have noticed as characterising the trade of these parts is exhibited in the London and St. Katharine's Docks, which are situated mainly in the parish of St. George's. People must be impressed with a sense of things being done on a large scale, when we have in one cellar six acres of port, sherry, and madeira, and under one roof

60,000 large casks of brandy, worth on an average, say, some £70 apiece. Besides the cellar just mentioned, there are eight others, not so large, but immense. I believe that almost all the wine that enters the port of London pauses here, and most of the brandy. The greater portion of the rum is received in the West India Docks. Of course, with such alcoholic temptations and opportunities, the greatest care is exercised to employ none but trustworthy men. Sometimes, however, appetite gets the better of conscience in the dock attendants. On one occasion this appetite was terribly avenged in the case of a greedy subordinate, who thrusting his head into a newly opened vessel of spirits with the intention of a drunken gulp, was thus choked and killed. The most strenuous pains are taken to prevent official intemperance. Indeed, I am informed that to be drunk on duty involves an *ipso facto* excommunication of any servant, however long he may have served, or however good his previous character. The question does not arise whether he shall be discharged; if he transgresses he discharges himself.

The vaults or cellars in which the wine is stored

are accounted one of the sights of London. They are, however, no more to be appreciated by a visit than London itself, inasmuch as the whole of a cellar cannot possibly be seen at once. You are provided with a round squat lamp at the end of a short flat stick, like a spoonful of fire, and are tramped, if you please, through miles of underground streets, on either sides of which are piles of casks. In the largest vault—which, like others, has its countless alleys laid with iron rails on which the casks are rolled—I am informed that they altogether reach the incredible distance of twenty-one miles. The alleys are, however, narrow. While in the midst of them you see only a little at a time. All along the route the ceiling is black with fungus, like that which is supposed to distinguish and commend a bottle of old port. Here wine is racked and blended. Great funnels like jellybags are filled with, say, port, which trickles brightly down from the tips of the bags, leaving the lees behind it. And very nasty they look.

Talking of unpleasant looking material in connection with eating and drinking, I may remark that the sugar, molasses, and treacle stores in the

Docks are anything but appetising. One day I was walking through the huge sheds on the ground floor where all this sweetstuff is lodged, and saw a parcel of men scraping the floor with hoes, much in the same way as the scavengers do the streets. And the mud they scraped up was very black. On my asking what they did with it, one of the superintendents told me it was going to be made into lollipops. Looking further, one could see many casks filled with this uninviting substance. However, whether it passes through the processes of the sugar refinery or not, the saccharine matter in the mess is made up into shapes nice-looking enough to children. Nothing is wasted from which sweets can be made. There is, though, one form of waste here which seems to me needless. One day I was standing on the church steps, and became conscious of what seemed to be an un-usual descent of huge smuts. The air was full of them. They spotted the church path and the street. It was a fall of black snow. I never saw such a murky downpour. We asked one another whence these dark flakes came. No chimney in the neighbourhood seemed to be smoking enough to account for them, and indeed they were unlike the usual London smuts. Presently, I found that they came from the Queen's Pipe, as it is called— a fierce furnace in which contraband tobacco is destroyed, and which just then was engaged in the destruction of some condemned tea. The atmosphere was still, and the result of this incremation powdered the neighbourhood. One of the Queen's Pipes—for there are two or three—is in the middle of St. George's, and such of my readers as are smokers can understand the pathetic air with which the man who tends it once told me he had consumed in a single smoking bout some five or six thousand pounds of shag tobacco. 'And ever so many cigarettes and cigars,' he added.

I asked him, in reference to the black storm I have mentioned, how he ever came to burn so much tea, and why it made such smuts? ' Tea, Sir,' he said, ' is a numb-burning thing; one can't get the fire into it.' That which is destroyed is such as has been mildewed, or is so bad that it is not worth having the duty paid on it. This, I am told, goes into the Queen's Pipe; but we use our own pipe seldom now.

The Docks abound with rats, and an army of about three hundred cats is employed to keep them down. Besides these you find dogs. Some little time ago I came on a famous one with her litter of puppies, close by the 'bowl' of our Queen's Pipe. Her owner volunteered a record of some of her performances in the rat-killing way, and fondly enumerated the number she had slain. But, like a true Englishman, he had his grievance. I learned that the Company does not pay for or provide the keep of the dogs, while it seems to be at the expense of extensive orders for cat's meat. I should have thought dogs would have needed food, while cats could have kept themselves. Some of these dogs are very sharp. I was one day walking through the Docks with my big black retriever, 'Jem,' when he was furiously attacked by a cur just outside the Brandy Delivery Office. Poor Jem is always unlucky in these encounters, since he is never prepared for an assault, and indeed is hopelessly penetrated with the belief that his size, weight, and general respectability of appearance ought to protect him. On this occasion he had been much exercised by the investigation of a quantity of treacle which had escaped on the quay from some burst cask, and which he was quite unable to analyse or account for. He had obviously met with nothing really resembling it before. It looked like some of the results obtained in connection with the killing of a pig, and as such he thought it well worth pausing to examine, but it made his nose and paws sticky. Thus he could not bring his mind to realise the charge of a dog much smaller than himself, and expressed his concern at the sudden change of the subject by tumbling over on his back and howling shamefully.

Beside the dogs and cats, there are men who get their living by clearing freshly unladen ships of rats. I believe that the charge for ratting a ship is £1. The rats are taken alive, and then sold for 2*d.* apiece to such as find amusement in killing them with dogs. As a couple of hundred rats are sometimes caught in one ship, the contracting catcher occasionally makes a good thing out of it.

Besides wine and brandy we land huge stores of ivory. In the early part of this year the result of discoveries of old accumulations of tusks by Livingstone made its appearance in a display of them, which at one sale realised, it is said, some £70,000. Divers of them were pronounced to be hundreds of years old. They covered a huge floor, and buyers came from all parts to secure them.

The wind is watched with much concern here by the dock-labourers, since upon it depends the due arrival of the ships, by the unlading of which they live. After a spell of east wind, which detains vessels in the Channel, the Docks are remarkably bare, while on its shifting, especially into the west, our waters are crowded as if by magic. And then the work presses. All sorts of cargoes, special and general, need to be bundled out as soon as the big ocean-going ships have crept slowly to their places alongside the quays. From my study-window I can see them, or at least their masts, towering above the roofs of some of the houses in the Ratcliff Highway, and moving towards their final berths, one after another, with a motion which from a little distance is hardly perceptible. What a change from some portions of their course! Talking of the arrival of ships and the diversities of sentiment in their voyage, I happened to be in the Docks when the 'Jefferson Borden' came in, on board of which a famous or infamous mutiny occurred on the high seas in April last. She was an American three-masted fore and aft schooner, deep in the water, being heavily laden with oilcake, which seemed to have saturated her deck. Indeed it was so greasy that I noticed several persons who traversed it carelessly slip down and have severe falls, which called forth an unsympathising laugh from the fringe of rough spectators who were not allowed to tread her planks. When she came alongside the quay I stepped on board. There, in the deck-house, lay the mutineers, wounded and ironed, with the marks around them of the bullets from the revolver with which the captain had protected his wife and himself. He was a quiet, slim, gentle spoken man, with a brown beard, and I had some conversation with him. The ship seemed certainly to have been undermanned, since there were only four men who, properly speaking, constituted the crew. Besides them were two mates, one the brother and the other the cousin of the captain ; and a steward, cook, and boy. One night three of the crew, after having gagged the boy, fell upon the two mates, killed and threw them overboard. Then one, a Finn, tried to entice the captain out of his cabin; but the captain missing his mates, and seeing that the man had something in his hand behind him— really the cruel iron bar with which the captain's brother had just been murdered—declined to come out till he had provided himself with a revolver. Then came the terrible time in which the captain, first with pistol-shots, which had plainly pitted the outside of the deck-house, drove the men within its shelter, and on their refusing to surrender, eventually fired into it upon them till they submitted to thrust their hands out of a little window in its side and be ironed. As I stood there the Thames Police swarmed in, and with stretchers and stern tenderness carried them off to the London Hospital. At that moment another ship came in, with a crew of negroes, and made fast alongside the American. They soon crowded the rigging, or peered over the bulwarks, to see the wounded mutineers borne off, thus witnessing one phase of a Nemesis which I could not help thinking, probably with injustice, set a grim lesson to as unpleasant countenanced a set of companions as any skipper ever found himself at sea with. But I dare say they were docile enough.

I was, indeed, struck with the example presented, in the landing of these mutineers, of the severity in judgment which sometimes pursues failure, or accompanies a sordid appearance. ‘Did you ever see three such rascally fellows?’ said a spectator to me, as the wounded murderers were being carried ashore. They were ill-looking, sure enough ; but if you were to take the three Graces and dress them in tarpaulins, and shut them up in a pigsty, and shoot their legs full of bullets, and tie their hands together, and lay them uncombed and unwashed on their backs for ten days, they would look, to say the least of it, ugly when drawn out into the sunshine. Pain and fear chiefly marked these poor fellows, though they were grievous malefactors. One of them cried out piteously as he was handed up the dock side. Their landing was a sad item of experience in that chance walk of mine along the quays.

The Docks are, however, an endless source of

entertainment and instruction to anyone gifted
with the least share of curiosity or observatiion,
and I must have a little more chat about them
before I pass on to some other prominent features
in the trade of these parts.   It is difficult to realise
the amount of labour and wealth represented by
the square plantations of bare masts upon which
we can look down from the summit of our church
tower.   They show like woods or copses in the
map of the estate of London.   In a much fuller
and more accurate sense than that in which the
phrase is generally used, the Docks are a world in
themselves, since they represent every corner of
the earth into which British enterprise has thrust
itself.   Those dull piles of white brick warehouses,
which discard every sentiment of decoration, and
fearlessly exhibit the ugly side of usefulness, are,
within, full of tropical products and appliances and
means of the most luxurious beauty and sumptuous
fare.   Here are stores of ivory and ebony.   Here
are the choicest cigars, the richest drugs, the
brightest dyes, the sweetest perfumes, and the
finest wines.   Here are landed and hence are
dispersed the accompaniments of perhaps the

costliest, most curious and exacting civilisation, and the busiest commerce to be found on the face of the globe. Here are pines from the West Indies, oranges from Seville, teas from China, masses of ice from Norway, and of marbles from Carrara, along with spices from Ceylon and ivory from Africa. Here, on these wharves, are heaped together for the day the most unlike though equally precious products of the earth, and yet many a man in walking through them would probably carry away a very slight impression of the business being carried on around him. Take our comparatively small docks, such as the London and St. Katharine's. I say comparatively small, as there are besides them the West India, Millwall, Surrey, &c. You perceive no bustle or prominent strain of labour within their limits, and would hardly believe that five or six thousand men are not unfrequently paid their wages at the close of the day. Their employment is, however, necessarily uncertain. The great bulk of them do not live here. Many of them—almost shiftless, without a trade, reminding one of Falstaff's recruits—come from all parts of London for the chance of a job;

and if the weather has been against the progress
of ships in the Channel, you may see hundreds of
these would-be labourers standing all the day idle
about the various entrances of the Docks.   Then a
shift of wind brings in a number of ships, and the
whole machinery of the place is suddenly in full
operation.   But it works smoothly, and it is only
after repeated visits that the magnitude and com-
plexity of the business transacted can be apprehended.   I am told that nothing strikes foreigners
more than the quiet methodical way in which
everything moves on here.   There is no shouting,
scolding, uproar, or excitement of any kind, as the
riches of the world are unfolded or poured out.
But go round the perfect little dock of St.
Katharine, with its hedge of hydraulic lifts steadily
disembowelling the vessels, which lie so close to
the shore that you might toss a halfpenny into
their holds when you look out of the top storey of
the warehouse which is absorbing the cargo.   Go
round this little dock.   Mount tier after tier of
floors; see even a single shipload of coffee, consisting
of about 10,000 bags or sacks, being repacked
and distributed ; or picture, if you can, the presence

of, say, £750,000 worth of indigo—which was the value of the amount being prepared for show in a single department when I went over it one day— and you will begin to perceive the largeness of the work in these parts, and admire the quietness with which it is carried on.

It must be remembered, however, that the surroundings of this dock represent but a small proportion of the storageroom used for merchandise in St. George's alone. After writing these lines I happened, on my way down to the Raines Schools on pastoral business, to fall in with our dock superintendent, who remarked that on one side of the Old Gravel Lane down which I was walking there were deposited I am afraid to say how many thousand tons of sugar, and 60,000 bags of coffee on the other. It is difficult to realise these quantities, much less what they represent ; for this bulk of coffee, enough one would think to keep London awake for a month, is only a passing deposit under one of divers roofs.

The floors of the indigo warehouses are, of course, of the deepest blue, and the sweepings sell for 2s. a pound. The indigo-brokers who come in from the City to examine the goods are the shrewdest, most experienced and patient judges of some kinds of colour in the world. They are mostly provided by the Company with a north light, like artists, in which to examine the various qualities of dyestuff laid out for them to inspect, and the prices of which range from about 3*s.* to 12*s.* a pound. Here, at a large tray, set where the shades of ultimate and latent dye may most easily be detected and distinguished, the broker potters away hour after hour, breaking, chipping, rubbing, peering into the lumps of indigo which, at a little distance, look like dark-blue coals. This inspection is, however, a dirty business, and the buyers or their clerks, who are well-paid experts, change their smart clothes before proceeding to transact it, and are provided in the dock warehouses with dressing-rooms in which to strip and wash when their day's work is done. They are, moreover, partly boarded as well as washed. On one of the floors is a dining-room, and a kitchen where a large charcoal fire suggests the sudden and perfect cooking of chops and beefsteaks.

The smell of some of the warehouses which

are loaded with spice is delicious. You may see
thousands of faggots of cinnamon, worth about £20
apiece, the making up and binding of which is
quite a trade. Each stick is separately examined.
The bark from which quinine is extracted arrives
in large cowskin packages, mostly with the hair
outside, like old-fashioned trunks. These, however,
are not corded, but sewn up with thongs, and cover
floor after floor. Talking of smells, I came one
day on ever so many waggon-loads of assafœtida,
and if anyone likes onions he ought not to object
to its odour. It is used as a condiment in Persia,
and a gentleman connected with the Docks who
happened to be accompanying me said it was
capital with beefsteak. His description of the
way in which a small portion of this pungent gum
should be rubbed on a hot plate when thus used
was most appetising. I do not think, however,
that it is offered to anyone furnished with a 'tasting
order.' This, as everyone knows, includes the
privilege of not only looking at the outsides of the
casks of port and sherry, but of boring into them,
and proving by another sense than that of sight
what they have within. The cellarman carries a

gimlet, and soon lets out a thin red spout of wine. This is, however, immediately checked with a little tap, by which, after steady blowing into it—a process that does not look nice, and rather suggests the idea that he is first taking a long pull himself —he fills divers of the largest wineglasses ever seen. These he empties on the sawdust floor with the carelessness of abundance when each visitor has taken a sip. Indeed, if visitors were to drink up all that might be offered to them, I fear that, however manifold the stores of casks may be, they would soon see double. Wine and spirit tasters in and about the Docks swallow nothing while engaged at their business, and retain the keenest susceptibility of palate. I cannot help thinking, though, that the complete testing of, say, wine, should involve some drinking of it ; and that the phrase, ' There is not a headache in a gallon of it,' should be verified by at least some approximate experiment. Perhaps, however, flavour conveys more to experts than to other men. There are gentlemen to whom a sensitive tongue is thus worth any money. They are at no expense to taste the choicest liquor, but are paid handsomely to sit all day, and sip, and smack their lips. Then they go home to dinner. It must be a dullish life.

My readers will be pleased to know that in connection with the Docks, at least with the London and St. Katharine's, there are compulsory night-schools for the boys, and that well-attended readings and entertainments are given in the winter to the servants of the company. Moreover, a gradually ascending scale of salary makes the position of a well-conducted official a comfortable and encouraging one. Commodious residences are provided for many of them, and anyone who, not knowing it, fancies that Wapping is a scene of coarse toil and rude debauchery, would be surprised to see the quiet pleasant river-side square which characterises the place. This square is well planted with trees, and skirted on two sides by handsome edifices which look on the Thames. These are mostly occupied by dock officers. In respect to other residents whose presence might be objectionable, pains are taken by the vestry of Wapping to discover and suppress any disorderly house within their jurisdiction. Beside these official residences there is excellent accommodation for artisans and others, erected by the company over which Sir Sydney Waterlow presides, and there has lately been built a small Board school for their children. Altogether, Wapping is one of the most respectable and well-conducted parishes in London. Curiously enough, the Orton family never lived there. Their house, which was pulled down this summer, was situated in St. George's, which extends nearly to the riverside. It latterly seems to have been used as an eating-shop, so that, as a man standing by it one day said to me, quite seriously, visitors might be able to say that they had dined in the room where 'Sir Roger' was born—a queer mixture of confused associations. This house stood near the Wapping entrance of the London Docks, and adjoined that in which it is said Lord Nelson got his outfit when he first went to sea. Both are now demolished to make way for warehouses, which promise to displace most of the old residences by the river-side in these parts. Indeed, the High Street of Wapping is gradually being skirted by enormous piles of these buildings, and before long few beyond the model lodging-houses of Sir Sydney Waterlow and the residences of the dock officers I have alluded to, will be left for domestic use. Hitherto this neighbourhood, though its Stairs are celebrated in song, has been supposed to be very little visited or traversed by the rest of the London world, especially the Western. Passengers by the Scotch steamboats have, however, always sailed from Wapping. And presently many residents in the West of London, especially those who live in the neighbourhood of the stations on the Metropolitan Railway, will be familiar with the railroad now rapidly approaching completion, which, running under the London Docks and cutting through St. George's and Wapping, will take them (possibly without change of carriage) to the Sydenham district and Brighton. This East London Railway will provide a very important outlet for the West as soon as the long-delayed work of boring under the Docks has been finished. The old Thames Tunnel already supplies a way for trains under the river, and gives access to Rotherhithe, which looks at us from the opposite bank. It is proposed also to provide a steam-ferry between the shores of the Thames at this spot. This, if provided, will be able to carry the loaded waggons which are now obliged to go round by London Bridge, some mile and a half off. As it is, I generally like to cross by a wherry, which provides a pleasant change from the usual modes of locomotion in London ; and in this case, when the place to be reached is Rotherhithe, affords the quickest, most obvious, though sometimes the least conventional means of access. The first time I went to dine with my old acquaintance, the rector of that parish—who is, indeed, a near neighbour, though the Thames lies between us—I landed on the beach, not far from his house, among a parcel of naked natives, like Captain Cook. It was high summer and low tide, and half the boys of Rotherhithe were bathing there.

But I must get back to the business of the Docks before I can recover any consciousness of doing my duty by a chapter which I have designated as 'Trades and Industries.' I don't know, though, what more I should have to say about them, except I went chatting on into the endless and changing daily experiences which characterise this phase of St. George's business, but which would weary my readers. I cannot, however, resist noticing the sense of relief with which one sees the bales of

Australian wool released from their restraint. They are made, of course, to take as little room as possible in the hold of the ship which brings them, and are thus before embarkation tightly nipped by enormous pressure and then bound with iron hoops, against which, like the cramped-up heart of the prince in one of Grimm's stories, they thrust and strain themselves, in impotent bondage, for long and weary months. At last the thus cruelly-laced bale is tumbled out of the ship's hold on one of the stone wharves which line the Docks. There it is presently laid upon its back by attendants, and a man sets it free with three or four smart and rapidly delivered blows of an axe. It is pleasant to see the immediate sense and hear the grunt of relief with which the iron-hooped truss of wool resumes its proper shape as its metal bonds are severed one by one and fly asunder. It soon becomes once more a plump and portly bale. Thus relieved, it is placed in the company of its fellows, who stand about comfortably, like aldermen with their waistcoats unbuttoned, and unsuspiciously awaits the visit of the wool-broker. He, however, at once takes advantage of its freshly recovered freedom.

by thrusting his hand into its stomach and pulling out its bowels. After this surprise and rough inspection by the brokers, the floors of the warehouses are knee-deep in wool, which has to be restored to the insides of the insulted bales by the servants of the Company before the goods are sold.

As I have remarked elsewhere, it is obvious that one of the chief features of the trade in these parts must be carriage. The stores accumulated in the warehouses which line the Docks, and which have been brought from all parts of the world in large quantities, have now to be dispersed. Much is sent away in barges, which, with an ugly outside and a roughish-looking crew, often contain a far more costly and delicate cargo than the ignorant passengers on the deck of a penny boat conceive. We have somehow associated the word 'bargee' with the coarsest trade and most unscrupulous manners. But, especially on the Thames, the lighterman holds a very responsible post. A gang of barges may represent not only a large sum of money, but most precious commodity. I was talking with an old 'bargee' one day who had so gnarled a face and such rugged hands that somehow I found myself assuming that he must be in charge of the roughest timber or stone, when he parenthetically observed that he was obliged to sleep on board, as his freight of silk was unusually delicate and valuable. We little realise the varied wealth hidden under the tarpaulin of those lumbering craft which drift in the tideway of the Thames, or which, as they lie at anchor, often seem to be under the sole charge of a little barking dog.

A considerable portion of the goods landed in the Docks is, however, dispersed by wheel and axle; and a 'carrier' here probably means a gentleman who has his country house, and comes in daily to offices hard by stables holding, say, a couple of hundred of the best draught-horses in London. Much business here, too, consists in the provisioning of ships, and especially in the furnishing of baskets and casks. Shops which make no very great display, and where one, ignorant of our trade, might think the neighbours chiefly got their brooms and mops, disclose unexpected relationship with distant parts of the world. I was talking with a neighbour once, who said, incidentally, he was rather hurried that morning, as he was sending off I forget how many thousand baskets to Buenos Ayres. A wholesale place like the border of the Thames exhibits at first many suchlike surprises to one who has been accustomed to associate shops merely with retail trade. The waggons which often block such thoroughfares as the Ratcliff Highway and Cable Street may be loaded with most precious or unexpected goods. I remember once my hansom being stopped by one which bore a mountain of cases, and noticing that they were marked 'Castor Oil'—a monstrous dose. We manufacture large quantities of cigars in what look like private houses. These are made by girls. It would only tire my readers if I were to dwell on the stores of ropes, sails, ships' lanthorns, &c. &c., which we provide and keep. The trade of St. George's is, however, speaking broadly, in a somewhat depressed state, since a chief feature of it is the refining of sugar. I have remarked that this branch of industry is at present, by the action of the French Government, which gives special facilities to its own producers and exporters of beetroot sugar, seriously injured. Large and costly refineries are standing still. And the complaint is not unjustly made, that St. George's does not just now thrive as it once did. But commerce still has its lively phases among us, as anyone may gather from my imperfect hints of the business that goes on in our midst. And it is in the nature of the Englishman to grumble.

It must not be supposed, however, though I have quoted the sugar-refineries as char cteristic of the trade of St. George's, that these r(present even the chief trades and industries of these Eastern parts. Perhaps the immediate prox'mity of two tall sugar-bakery chimneys to our ch irch makes me think more of them than of others. In fact, the East of London abounds with large and important manufactories, and has done its part in the great manufacturing and commercial development of these latter days. Such a statement may seem superfluously true to those who live in this part of the metropolis; but as the East—partly through the influence of begging-letters, some of which falsely set forth Easterners as the scum of the metropolis; partly through the unconscious ignorance of those who live in the West, and who are loosely considered, I suppose, the chief exponents of London observation and thought—has been looked down upon, at the best, almost as a crowd of poor lodging-houses inhabited by the poorest servants of the West, I must be allowed, at the risk of repetition, to draw my reader's attention to some other phases of the industry that characterises it, besides those to which I have already referred, and which mostly concern the immediate neighbourhood of the Docks.

It is, as it were, a manufacturing city in itself, though its proximity to the colossal centre of commerce, known as the 'City' of London, has so dwarfed it that people in general have very erroneous ideas of its industrial importance. It is, moreover, though counted as distant, not far enough from the West to appear in due perspective. Large provincial towns, such as Leeds and Sheffield, stand out distinctly in the manufacturing scenery of England. Everyone sees and recognises their commercial individuality and importance. Perhaps this is clearer from the fact of their being characterised by special manufactures, such as woollen cloth and cutlery; still their prominence is partly due to their distinctiveness. Were they suburbs of London the case might be somewhat different.

Now East London, though attached to the metropolis, and forming a part of it, is in some respects almost a separate centre of industry. It is poor by the side of the concentrated luxury of the West, and the riches of the City, but not poor in the sense of being a depraved and pauperised section and servant of the metropolis. Its industrial products are spread far beyond London. True, it is not characterised by the production of any one article of commerce which gives it an exclusive place among centres of industry ; but many who look on it as representing merely the poor and toilsome side of London, ministering mainly to the wants of the metropolis, would, I think, be interested in realising to some slight extent how widely its manufacturing industry is felt.

It would be impossible for me, in a chapter touching the Trades and Industries of the East, to do more than point to a few examples of what I mean. Take, for instance, the chemical works which distinguish the East. I am thinking now of one firm, which owns the largest distillery of gastar in the world, and has branch establishments not only in other parts of England, but in France, Belgium, and Russia. One feature of its work is the creosoting of railway sleepers, which it turns out at the rate of some 30,000 a week. It moreover makes pitch, naphtha, &c., and transforms what used to be waste into material for some of the most beautiful colours used in textile fabrics. The central works of this firm cover some 17 acres; and it is obvious that here we have an aspect of East London industry, which shows an independence of what Easterners are I think justly touchy about, mere ministration to the rest of London.

Take again 'matches.' The match-making trade is capable of such subdivision as enables much to be done at the homes of those employed in it. All recollect the irruption of match-makers, when it was proposed to lay a tax upon these common articles of domestic use. They would have been equally remonstrant if the centre of match-making had been hundreds of miles away; but because it happened to be in the East of London, those engaged in it were able to make a personal demonstration against the proposed tax

under the eyes of the Legislature, which for once
saw, at short range, some of the toes of this centi-
pede nation that objected to be pinched. And
their unexpected presence was, it seemed to me,
counted as a revelation of the poor servants of the
metropolis. Not a bit of it. They are really
fellow-servants, with the rest of industrial London,
to the realm. We make matches for the whole
kingdom. When I say that the firms of the
Messrs. Palmer, Bryant & May, Bell & Black,
&c. &c., are situated in the East of London, I give
another instance of one of the independent industries which mark these parts. Perhaps, however,
the match-making business, or rather the manufacture of wooden match-boxes, in the East of
London, has done as much as anything to create
an impression of our indigence. Some years ago
a piteous picture was drawn of this trade, especially
of the share which children had in it in the homes
of working-people. There is nothing more fragile
and transitory than the common wooden box
which holds lucifers. It would perhaps be difficult
to think of any article in large use which could be
more easily made. It requires very small skill in

its manufacture. Thus the children of poor people in the neighbourhood of the match manufactory have a chance of earning a few extra halfpence, and what is counted by some as a sign of depressed and depressing industry really indicates a phase of honest work which enables the unskilled to add to their means. Anyhow, the manufacture of matches, carried on largely in the East of London, shows a form of industry which is widely felt, and helps to deliver us from the charge of being a sort of pauperised hangers-on to the metropolis. Look into any small shop in any of the villages of England, look on the shelf of any farmhouse or cottage throughout the land, and you will find a sign of one of the trades and industries of the East of London.

Pass from the most fragile to the strongest products of the hand of man, and ask where some of the most ponderous and perfectly-finished armour-clad ships of war in the world come from, and you will find that they have been built in East London. I wonder what the yearly expenditure in wages alone is in the yards of, say, the Messrs. Samuda, who have furnished ironclads far and wide.

Take the trade of another Parliamentary firm, which, with the last-mentioned, represents the Tower Hamlets in the House of Commons: I mean the jute manufactories of Messrs. Ritchie & Sons. There we have another large example of East London industry. I have been informed, but I really forget, how many thousand yards of jute-cloth this firm turns out daily; but it is only an item in the mass of testimony which goes to exhibit the East of London as one of the great districts of industry in the land, and one which worthily takes its place, not as dependent on the rest of the metropolis, but as sharing with it the honour of being the greatest centre of work and commerce in the world.

It would indeed be hard if we did not find London itself one of our best customers for much that we produce: take, for instance, the great wholesale clothing establishments which characterise the East. We cannot of course boast of the most fashionable or expensive tailoring shops, but we make immense quantities of clothing, much of which is sold and worn in London. And the manufacture of silk, which some twenty years ago.

had certainly fallen to a low ebb in these parts, has, I am given to understand on good authority, seen a revival.   I should weary my reader if I were to go through the list of trades which thrive in the East.   We have all sorts, including boat-building, coach-making, paper-staining, distilling, soap-making, and braid-weaving ; and even Birmingham has not the questionable monopoly of providing cheap guns for bloodthirsty African tribes.   These weapons, of which I have seen heaps in the course of manufacture not far from my house, are certainly doubtful to look at, though I assume they are 'proved.'   I am inclined to believe that the Ashantees were armed with them in our late 'little war,' and that such of our men as were hit were wounded from British barrels, if not from some that had long lain in the Tower.   I came one day on a number of Tower muskets which had been sold by the Government, and were, I was told, on their way to Africa.   Your Ashantee, at least your East African warrior, is, they say, glad enough to use the old flint-lock 'Brown Bess.'   I bought one for a few shillings, as a weapon fast becoming a curiosity, together with a heavy pair of large flint horse-pistols which had been laid up in the Tower after the Peninsular War, and which, when dis-charged, make as much noise and smoke as small cannons. Talking of cannons, we could at St. George's supply anyone who wanted them with every variety of ship's guns : I do not mean such as are used in warfare, but those carried by mer-chant vessels for the purpose of signalling. I see them in shop-windows, along with small anchors and patent logs, which last look like spinning-baits for sharks. In these parts, moreover, we have large cork manufactories, where life-buoys and belts may be had in abundance.

In respect to the work of the labourer and artisan, this immediate neighbourhood differs from that with which I became well acquainted during my sojourn at St. Luke's, Berwick Street. The bulk of trades in that locality are unknown here. There we turned out enormous quantities of the most highly-finished and skilled hand-work that is associated with luxurious civilisation. Here our work is good, but more severely useful. There we made jewel-boxes and dressing-cases, cut dia-monds, strung pearls, painted church-windows, sewed fine clothes for the 'upper ten thousand,' provided lathes for amateur turners, and manufactured all kinds of curious projectiles for the most elaborate and scientific sportsman. There we produced thousands of artificial teeth and wax-flowers; we made sausage machines, window-blinds, fiddles, and lasts. Here we load and unload great ships, drive heavy vans, stitch sails, twist ropes, tug at lumbering barges, sort, store, and distribute mixed cargoes in warehouses. Every kind of work here, even the commonest, is associated with interests that are obviously large; and, as I have remarked elsewhere, I think that the consciousness which it involves of contact with the ends of the earth is not without effect on the character of the people. They are, I think, more large and cosmopolitan in their views and conversation than my old friends at St. Luke's, who are imprisoned for long periods in close streets and rooms, with heads bent over some small process in the skilled ministrations of artificial life. Here most seem to have seen something of the world, and disclose unexpected experiences in conversation. I think this moment of three men who are daily engaged about our church and churchyard, and who might any morning be seen together at our gate. One was for many years guard of a popular mail-coach; another, apropos to some remark of mine one day, incidentally showed that he was familiar with Constantinople; and when I had been here some time, I found that the third had twice been round the world.

Another contrast may be seen in what certainly appears to me the superior physique of the East-erners. The nature of our work (I am thinking now especially of St. George's) takes us much into the air. I have repeatedly been struck with the healthy looks of our children; and children, if they survive carelessness in nursing, are sensitive sanitary meters. We have more colour in the cheek and lip, and more laughter in the eye, than some I have seen elsewhere. The notion of the poor in the East of London being a white-faced stunted race is a mistake, at least as far as the neighbour-hood of the Docks is concerned. If you were to weigh the first hundred working-men that passed your door in these parts, against such a hundred in (say) Soho, I am persuaded that we should bring down the scale. But these considerations belong more properly to a chapter in which I shall try to notice something in respect to the physical condition of the people in these parts, than one in which I ought to confine myself to observations on the trades in which they are engaged. The dwellers in the East of London in general are, as I have observed, engaged largely in manufactures which concern the country at large ; and in respect to the particular locality in which my work lies, the trades, as my readers will have seen, are determined in great measure by the fact that we are among the first to receive and handle the riches of the earth which are poured into London. Our contact with distant places is fresh, our people are related to sailors, our estimate of commerce is formed before the wholesale importation of goods is divided into the many rills of retail trade. The main stream of business, like the Thames which carries it, flows through our midst ; and while we see it bringing varied and abundant stores to the great city on whose skirts we live, the space afforded by the Docks and River, and the nature of much of the work which they exact, delivers us from the closeness and pressure which characterise most parts of London, and certainly presents a result which contrasts remarkably with those central districts in the metropolis which I know best. We have more room, in and out of doors; and as the wind is frequently in the East, we send our smoke West, and see the sun through a thinner cloud of blacks than if we lived in some fashionable streets where the sky is yellow from the fumes of a million fires.

The ebb and flow of the tide has, moreover, I fancy, some effect upon the atmosphere in these parts. However still the air may be, yet the constant movement of a large volume of water must more or less affect it. The River is, indeed, my chief source of refreshment. When weary, I have again and again betaken myself to the Thames Tunnel Pier, which is ten minutes' walk from my door, and had an airing to Blackwall and back for a few halfpence in one of the Woolwich boats. This little run is, moreover, always full of incessant change and interest, the varying states of the tide ever presenting some fresh aspect of river life. Sometimes when the wind is strong, and many red-sailed barges are making the most use of it, the course of the river steamers is critically tortuous or intermittent. The experts who steer them, or rather the captains who direct the helmsman, are wonderfully clever in dodging other craft. The success with which they calculate on barely shooting between two approaching barges in full sail is such that one ceases to think of the mischief that might follow a collision. The chief cause of accident, however, arises from carelessness or ignorance on the part of those in boats. The way in which a parcel of cockneys will sometimes row in a crowded river and a strong tideway almost exceeds belief. Were it not for the wakeful skill of the steamboat captains, skiffs would be incessantly run down during the summer months. I have known a steamer pulled up short, not without maledictions on the part of its crew, twice in a few hundred yards on a June evening, when your cockney is disporting himself on the water. Minor accidents, however, continually happen which are nowhere recorded. Some of the larger ships on leaving the Thames are occasionally, it seems to me, very heedless. The other day I was standing on one of our piers when a foreign steamer, an iron screw, came tearing down and fouled a brig at anchor. The steamer apparently got the worst of it, for the brig's nose scraped a portion of her bulwarks off, which came splashing down into the water. But she paused only, it would seem, to be assured that no man had been dragged overboard, and then steamed off as hard as she could, with a volley of impotent oaths after her. These sort of scrapes, however, happen only with the least reputable vessels which are ill-found and under-manned. The larger ships are handled with excessive pains. See how carefully one of these will back out the Docks at the top of the tide before she is picked up by her attendant tug, and towed down the Thames. It is fine to see a dozen or so of these being dragged towards the sea, when the floodtide has just turned, and the river brims.

The Blackwall Pier is, I think, the best from which the Londoner may see the traffic of the Thames. It is certainly reached by a railway which has some of the dirtiest and shabbiest stations and carriages to be found anywhere, and thus the contrast presented when the door of the Blackwall Terminus has been passed is the more striking. You exchange in a moment its dingy interior for the view of a grand bend in the river, alive with a crowd of red-sailed barges and other craft, through which a few big ships proceed slowly, like oxen among sheep. To the right the masts of the vessels in the West India and Millwall Docks show like a larch plantation in the winter-time. Both ways there is a long view down the Thames.

This spot was once chosen as a likely site for a temple of whitebait, but the hotel is now converted into an Emigrant Depôt. With its bow-windows commanding a finer prospect than 'The Ship' at Greenwich, it is now a hive of swarming emigrants, at least just before each shipload of them is despatched. The large balconied dining-room has exchanged the 'purple and fine linen' of its white cloths and coloured wineglasses for a number of plain bare deal tables.

I must say a word about this, as it is indeed in some measure characteristic of the business that goes on at this end of London. Not only are we in contact with the uttermost parts of the earth by means of the merchandise which we receive from thence, but this depôt is our door of departure for New Zealand. I have frequently to sign the papers of those who sail hence. The first day I visited it the dining-room was filled with a crowd of hungry emigrants waiting for dinner, and the air with the odour of its advent. They sat in messes of eight or ten, to each of which was a captain, who kept his nose steadily pointed towards the door through which the smell came.

Presently a signal was given, and each disappeared, receiving a ticket as he passed out. With this he descended to the kitchen, returning in a minute or two, mostly grinning, and bearing a large brown oval dish, divided in the middle. One half was filled with roast-beef and the other with potatoes. There was enough and to spare for all. 'They waste a lot,' said one of the officials. But I don't know; it seemed to be appreciated. 'Ah,' remarked a country-looking fellow to me, with his cheek bulged with a huge bite, and a twinkle in his eye, 'I wish, sir, they would let me stay here for a month.' 'Rare good victuals,' said another.

' I believe you,' added a third ; ''Tain't allus we've had a bellyful of cooked meat every day.'

The emigrants are fed and taken to New Zealand free of charge, excepting £1 each for ' bedding-money ' for those over twelve, and 10s. each for those under that age. I was struck with the air of confidence displayed by most. They were leaving the old country with less regret than I liked to see, though some of the elders looked sad. The majority were labourers. The officials told me that on the arrival of the ship at its destination they were for some time lodged in a depôt free of expense, but that they were generally engaged at once, or soon fetched away by friends.

The sleeping arrangements at the depôt prepare the emigrants for their inevitable crowding on board-ship. The married couples have each a berth to themselves, but dozens of these sleep in what would be called, on shore, the same apartment. Their discomfort, to use the mildest word, especially during the first week of the voyage, must be extreme. The single men and women are of course kept scrupulously apart, and their berths, especially those of the former—which were

22 inches wide, and separated by a wooden division
some 6 inches high—looked unpleasant enough.
However, free carriage and food can hardly be
expected to be luxurious. Some of the men wore
red-carpet slippers, which were an odd finish to an
earth-stained suit of fustian or corduroy. Divers,
however, had on their 'Sunday' clothes. The
vessels are fine-looking and roomy. But the
'roominess' of a ship, like that of any other place,
is comparative, being determined by the number
it is made to hold. Several of them were waiting
their turn in the Docks hard by, and sticking their
bowsprits over the quays in that long masted line
which fringes the land in these parts, and to which
the dirty Blackwall Railway ministers with incessant trains. The depôt associated with this at
Plymouth sends emigrants to Sydney, Adelaide,
and New Zealand. This at Blackwall is a point of
embarkation for New Zealand alone, and has seen
the departure of seventeen thousand emigrants
from May 11th, 1874, to August 7th in this
year, which gives an average of more than a thousand a month. I found divers Scotch and German
families awaiting the next ship. It looks as if

New Zealand were filling up fast, since this is only part of the human stream which is incessantly being poured into it from Europe.

The training of carrier-pigeons forms, apparently, part of the business of the East of London. I was waiting for the boat the other day at Blackwall, and found a young girl with a basket of birds. Each bird had a small compartment and lid to itself. Every five minutes, by the station clock, the girl opened a lid and let out a bird, which after flying up and taking an airy glance, made off home. Next day, the girl said, she was going to let the basketful loose farther down the river. Anyone leaving London by the Great Eastern Railway must have noticed the numerous slight structures, used for pigeons, on the roofs of the poorer houses which skirt the line. We have a good many of these birds about us, and a colony of them has this year established itself in the tower of our church. This their ' castle in the air ' is also shared by numerous sparrows, which I think have increased in number since they found out the water-pans with which we supply our cocks and hens. It is difficult for them to get what they want out of the Docks, for the sparrow must sit at the edge of his liquor in order to drink, and a sheer descent of some 10 feet of quay-side wall puzzles him, however thirsty he may be.

In looking back over the present chapter on the Trades and Industries of the East of London, I see I have omitted to state that we are conspicuous for our manufacture of the best fireworks, which we supply to various parts of England, sending with them, if needed, experts to superintend and direct their displays. Indeed it would seem that even the expedition of the Prince of Wales to India is furnished with them from these regions, and that the sparks which will dazzle the eyes of our fellow-subjects in our Eastern dominions will have been prepared in the Eastern portion of our metropolis.

But, whether the need be small or great, anyone wanting such things had much better buy them here at first-hand. Last year, while away for my summer vacation in the country, I contributed a box of mixed fireworks at a village-school feast, and it was surprising not only how much fire, noise, and smell we got out of a pound's worth, but what a variety of elaborate wheels and rockets came out of our parcel. They were most vehemently applauded by the rustic lads and lasses, and left an impression on their minds that a place which could produce such brilliant fabrics must be altogether a dazzling and beauteous realm—which is complimentary to the East of London.

THE parish — St. James's, Westminster — in which I had worked for 15 years before I came to St. George's was, under the supervision of successive rectors, well provided with schools. But when I came here I found no school attached to the Mother Church beside that associated with Raine's Charities—of which more presently. True, there is within the limits of the part of the parish specially under my charge a District Church school, carried on with much spirit and success in arches under the Blackwall Railway. But even if this were large enough to take in the untaught of its immediate neighbourhood, its situation ought to condemn it. The ceiling of the school-room is the floor of the railway. Every two or three minutes a train rushes overhead with a scream and a roar that obliterates the voice of teacher and scholar. It may be that those who study under these noises.

grow used to them, but it is hardly well to become so used to a bad thing as not to notice it. For it must be bad, even though it may compel some children to read aloud with special effort and distinctness. Too much praise, however, cannot be given to those who have done a good work under such great difficulties.

Having been long deeply interested in education, and having indeed been the moving cause in the erection of successful schools at St. Luke's, Berwick Street, I felt aghast at the apparently inadequate provision at St. George's for the elementary education of my poor neighbours, and was not sorry to hear that a Board-school was about to be built in that part of the parish still ecclesiastically attached to the Mother Church. Some of my new friends, indeed, disliked the prospect of it, but literally one quarter of an hour's observation convinced me that a great hope of the parish lay in its provision.

One week-day afternoon, at three o'clock, when the existing schools were at work, I walked round the site of the projected Board-school with my pencil and note-book in my hand. In fifteen minutes I counted 232 children, apparently of an

age to attend school, sitting on doorsteps or playing in the street. That settled the question in my
mind, and I saw with joy the walls of the new
school-rooms begin to rise. The building was
designed eventually to accommodate 1,200 scholars,
but since doubts had been expressed as to the need
of so large an establishment, only half was built to
begin with. When the half was completed, though
as yet unused, I went over it, and rejoiced again to
think that some at least of the little ones now
rambling around would be taught, and in light
wholesome rooms. As soon as the school was
opened the children poured into it, till it was brim
full. One afternoon, while there were 650 children
present in this school, which was constructed to
hold only 600, I made another circuit with my note-
book and pencil. On this occasion I counted, in
six minutes, 72 children still sitting on doorsteps
or playing in the street, within bow-shot of the
school. I need hardly say that the second half of the
building was proceeded with speedily. It has, however, not 'filled' as it ought. Their work may be
difficult, but I do not think that those officials whose
business it is to sweep the streets for scholars

realise what they have to do. It strikes me that they are more ready to meddle with existing denominational schools than to forage for those under the Board.

Statistics and disputes about the procedure of the London School Board have been so plentifully set before the public that I will not attempt to furnish any fresh information of that kind about the matter. I am constrained, however, to state my belief that in the end the School Board must swallow up, or leave dry, all, or almost all, the common primary schools in the metropolis. No doubt there are cases in which the Board-school supply is provokingly in excess of the demand, and a clergyman who at much pains and cost has built Church schools in his district may be pardoned for some expressions of sharpness or dismay at seeing a newly-created power come into his parish, and not only provide buildings better than his, but outbid him in the market for teachers and their assistants. The first movements of a revolution must pinch, press, or put out somebody, but I think it was high time for Government to take up the cause of education as it has done.

It is all very well to talk of *voluntary* schools, but the word suggests a spontaneity of support which is hardly warranted by facts. People forget, or do not know, the strenuous, incessant, and even humiliating pains which the promoters of voluntary schools, mostly clergymen, have been at to set them up and keep them going. When, *e.g.*, I first went to St. Luke's, Berwick-street, I found a mixed school held in the dark rooms under the church. It cost such and such a sum yearly. My friend, the rector of the parish, who had supplied this money, told me that if I established better schools he would allow me towards their maintenance the subsidy which had been granted towards the old mixed school out of the central educational fund of the parish; and he added a condition that any subscription then being received from the district parish of St. Luke's should be handed over to the central fund. And what did it amount to? From a population of between nine and ten thousand the beggarly sum of a guinea and a half was all, and that represented two subscribers.

That fact has since taught me much. It was monstrous that in so large a portion of St. James's,

Westminster, virtually none had cared to help with their money in the cause of primary Church education. However, I accepted the conditions, and having secured an old chapel, converted it, at a considerable expense, into school-rooms, in which, though I say it myself, some good educational work was done. Before I left, and when I left, the schools were full and thriving. We added, moreover, a master's house and playground. These schools were certainly a success.

But the toil and time given to the whole business were such as those only know who have undertaken and carried out such a work. I did not indeed anywise grudge my pains, for the idea of a London School Board was not then born. But when I think of the large number of people who were asked to give, and gave nothing, though they were such as the friends of Church education had reason to look to for aid, and when I remember that my case was only one of hundreds, and that many parsons half wore out their hearts in straining themselves to provide elementary schools by sheer dint of pertinacity, I cannot help a chuckle at seeing the educational net thrown over this recusant section of the public, who are now compelled by the action of the London School Board to put their hands into their pockets.

This compulsory subscription to educational purposes, obnoxious to many, presents itself in a special light to those who have felt what it is to establish and support national schools. At St. Luke's we eventually raised by small solicited subscriptions some thirty pounds annually from the district, but this came in drops, and some of the largest makers of money in the place steadily refused to give anything. Our help came chiefly from the same kind hands as we looked to for support in all Church work, and who were in many cases unconnected with the district. It is true that we did thus carry the schools on, and keep a balance on the right side, but the bulk of the people, who by residence and business were most concerned in the well-being of the district, contributed nothing, though repeatedly asked to do so. The time had arrived for these, and such as these, to be compelled to do their share towards so important a work as that of national elementary education. It was intolerable that the parson should be expected to dun for money to educate the people, and have, in many instances, donations to the schools looked upon as personal aid to or patronage of himself. And it was monstrous that a state of things which drove him to scrape, and beg, and screw, and subject himself to endless refusals should be dignified by the name of the Voluntary System. Barring a few liberal hearts who always responded to the mere announcement of a want, donors had to be hunted out and besieged with all that machinery of petition, pressure, and entreaty from which the soul recoils. And for what? For so crying a need as national elementary education.

It was therefore with a sentiment of relief and satisfaction that shortly after my coming to St. George's I saw the walls of a fine Board-school creeping up, and knew that throughout the metropolis the saddle had at last been put upon the right horse, and that the parson, in respect at least to this item of needful work, was no longer compelled to exhibit himself to his parishioners and the public as a beggar. It would be difficult to say how much we parsons have been injured morally by the habit of begging contracted in the strain to provide and support schools for the poor amongst whom we minister.

I am inclined to think that though some schools are still kept afloat by the parson, we are witnessing the expiring phases of his enforced pertinacity in this respect. Before long Board-schools must represent the primary education of the metropolis. People will not eventually yield to the appeals of the 'voluntary' school collector while they are compelled to pay taxes for education. Habit and respect for individual clergy may keep the old order alive here and there for a few years. The old voluntary ship may thus float a little while, but it is settling down, however assiduously its crew may work at the pumps. New men, not inheriting the educational sentiments and obligations of the past, will be found unwilling to commit themselves to efforts which are virtually hopeless, and it will be a day of wholesome relief to the clergy when they can generally realise that the old order has given place to new.

Of course I am well aware of the drawbacks, or supposed drawbacks, to their good estimation of

Board-schools involved in the fact that the clergy are forbidden to teach the scholars of the Board-school in their parish, and that, especially, the reading of the Bible is left to the superintendence of the master. This regulation not only hurts the feelings of men who know that the nation has mainly had to thank them for its best primary educational work in the past, but in one aspect it is an absurd waste of power to decline the help of those who have long taught conscientiously, and know how to teach so as to put fresh warmth and interest into dull educational routine. But whether the conduct of late educational legislation has been somewhat bungled, or whether the parsons themselves have shown in some instances too much acrimony of opposition to the measures in question, so it is ; and it would be well for such as kick against the pricks to see, even at the eleventh hour, whether they cannot make the best of what they think to be a bad bargain. If the clerical world had not risen with vehemence against the educational parliamentary proposals the case might have been different, and even now it is possible that some modifications of the existing rules may be eventually introduced if the clergy moderate some of their antagonism to Board-schools.

I, for one, am however very much inclined to doubt whether the clerical direction of the religious teaching in our elementary Church schools in London has really provided such spiritually righteous results as some would credit it with. Individual instances of wholesome religious teaching have of course been seen again and again in connection with most national schools, and, especially in the days when children were examined in their religious knowledge by the Government Inspector, astonishing accuracy in the details of Biblical history and Church doctrine was exhibited by many of them ; but the great bulk of those children of the working classes who have long been thus sedulously taught the Bible and the catechism have grown up wholly indifferent to at least the services of the Church. When I first went to St. Luke's there was a huge gallery at the west end of the building, into which the children of the St. James's national schools were trooped every Sunday, and had been so trooped for I do not know how many years. There were about six hundred of them. And thus, since the body of the church was but thinly attended, the preaching there was like addressing a rookery across a field.

This arrangement was altered very shortly after I began my ministrations in the parish of St. James's. The St. James's children were provided with a special service in their own room, half of the gallery being removed, and though our own Sunday-school scholars still sat aloft and joined in the prayers, I always sent them out before the sermon, allowing only such of the elders as chose to do so to remain in the body of the Church. But the sight of those six hundred children perched in the gallery on Sundays, and the consciousness that they were regularly instructed in the Bible and the catechism during the week, coupled with the knowledge that not one in a hundred ever attended the services of any church as soon as their school course was over, has presented and penetrated me with an instance of the apparently small religious results obtained in a school carefully superintended, and taught by an able and pious master. And this was only an example of many, I may say most, denominational schools, for

I am persuaded that the shortcoming I speak of has been exhibited among Nonconformists as well as Church people. Surely it is hardly worth while to make an outcry about the discontinuance of a system which, as a means of indoctrinating children with at least those religious sentiments that result in their after attendance at public worship, has been so deplorable a failure.

As to the dreaded effect of Board-schools leading children, by reason of the undenominational way in which the Holy Scriptures are there taught, to grow up indifferent to the observances of religion, the system has not been tried long enough for any one to form an opinion. But it could, in this respect, be hardly more barren than that which it supersedes. And indeed I am inclined to believe that children may, as they pass into manhood, become more interested in spiritual things, as they have not been strenuously plied in childhood with compulsory technical religious teaching. They will still be taught to read the Bible, and when they have left school for some time will not be conscious of that formulated sediment of doctrinal instruction which now tends to lead them to think that

they have already been taught what the Church
has to teach, and which is in their minds associated
with week-day instruction—which at the time was
more or less uninteresting or distasteful—and compulsory session on a hard bench on Sundays in
a hot gallery during a sermon which they did not
understand.   A boy who has been thus technically
taught 'religion' in the week, and compelled for
five or six years to sit every seventh day for a
couple of hours on a deal form while the service
has been going on, is not likely afterwards to view
that service with interest. If this long-pursued
system has been a training up of children in
the way that they should go, and if it is to be
tested by their after attendance at public worship,
Solomon's estimate of the result has not been
worthy of his reputed wisdom.

In respect to the present educational measures
of the Government, I cannot resist the conviction that they will have to be much modified.
Direct compulsory education will never be generally
accepted or acceptable in England. Its reputed
success, especially in Prussia, is no earnest of its
success here. There it forms part of a severe

paternal government ; but here, if it is not a piece of new cloth in an old garment, it is radically opposed to the strongest sentiments of that class to which it is chiefly intended to be applied. Already a feeling of irritation at the fining of parents for the non-attendance of their children at school is spreading, and possibly a few more turns of the compulsory screw may bring about a deep and extended resistance to the direct compulsory system. As it is, direct compulsion cannot really be said to be generally applied. There are obviously large numbers of children in our streets who are untouched. The school visitors cannot or will not lay hold of them. If they cannot, the system seems simply to fail ; and if they put forth fresh energy, and do succeed in netting any large numbers of those who are now allowed by their parents to run the streets, hauling them into school, and extorting their fees by legal process, I am persuaded that this direct compulsory system will be seen to break down ignominiously. The present Government instrument of education is still on the anvil, and it will want much turning and hammering before it takes its final shape.   We are as yet only beginning the work.

The chief provision hitherto made in St. George's for the education of the poor is seen in 'Raine's Charities,' which, some 150 years ago, long before the revival in national education, assisted by the parochial clergy, was begun, and when Board-schools were undreamt of by the most advanced seer into the future, provided for the instruction and clothing of 50 boys and 50 girls. These are taught in solid red 'Queen Ann' brick buildings down Old Gravel Lane.   Outside the school are set figures of the boy and girl of the period, and a tablet declares the spirit of Raine in the words, 'Come in and learn your duty to God and man'—excellent advice, which it would be well for any school managers to take as their motto, and put forth as the true purpose of all education.   Along with these charity schools Mr. Raine founded, hard by, an asylum for the boarding, clothing, and teaching of 40 girls, to be chosen from the girls' school, and for four years instructed in and fitted for domestic service.   These charities Mr. Raine placed under the government of a board of some 40 trustees. And he added this kindly direction, that when the girls came of suitable age to be married, two every year should be presented with a marriage portion of £100 each, provided they could produce satisfactory testimonials from the masters or mistresses of the households where they had lived of piety, industry, and continuance in the principles of the Episcopal Church of England, and presented to the trustees as suitors young men also well recommended as members of the Church of England, and living in one of the 'parishes of St. George, Middlesex; Saint Paul, Shadwell; or St. John, Wapping;' the preference being given to a man living in St. George's.

Here worked a paternal spirit, though Mr. Raine was no father, but, as he states in his will, kept himself unmarried that he might have enough to spare for the poor children of his parish without impoverishing his relations. This conscientious and kindly Churchman left also behind him a large number of rules and regulations for the application of his generosity, and among them a singular order for the disposal of the marriage portion.

As of course more than two of the 'asylum' girls might annually be found ready to fulfil the conditions I have referred to, it is further directed that the marriageable maidens should, not more than six at a time, draw lots for the £100.

This drawing for the marriage portion has naturally become an institution at St. George's. It takes place on the 1st of May and 5th of November, when those who have been so fortunate as to draw prizes six months before are married, with some pomp, in the parish church. These days are kept ceremoniously. Peals are rung upon the church bells, the children, accompanied by the trustees and other officials, march through the streets with banners and nosegays, and the trustees and their friends dine (at their own cost) in the large room of the asylum. The children are on these occasions plentifully fed out of the funds of the Charity, and a special dinner is provided for the newly-married couple, who in the course of the evening present themselves before the trustees and their guests in the large room to receive congratulations, good advice, and a purse containing 100 new sovereigns from the chairman.

It is altogether a busy day. First comes the procession to the church, then the marriage of the girl who drew the prize six months before; then, accompanied by suitable addresses, the drawing of lots by those who hope to be married six months later; then the children's dinner; and then, involving the presentation of the marriage portion, the trustees' entertainment, which last entails a long list of toasts.

The real business of the Charities has however in process of time become so cumbrous, question-able, and complicated that the trustees have lately applied to the Endowed Schools Commissioners for a new scheme which shall enable them to make the best use of the funds at their disposal. As I write, this scheme is in preparation, and I cannot tell what shape it will assume. But while it is to be presumed that it will grant much satisfactory power to the governing body of the Charities, I hope it will not present any deviation from the main principles which have hitherto guided the trustees. It had, however, become obvious to them that some changes and modifications in the conduct of the schools and asylum were needed, and this seemed a suitable time at which to seek the co-operation of the Commissioners.

These Charities have done very good work in their day ; they are intimately associated with the civil and religious life of St. George's, and are capable of being rendered more serviceable to the parishioners than they have ever been. But we have become hide-bound. Some of our rules and customs are absurdly objectionable and severe. The girls, *e.g.*, in the asylum, who are there being fitted for domestic service, have had no corporate holydays, being permitted to visit their parents rarely, in driblets—and then only for a day—while their parents were never allowed within the walls of the asylum. The girls, moreover, have not been accustomed to be taken out for a walk, having been kept strictly within the walls of the building and its premises. Indeed the rules of a nunnery could hardly be more strict about their relationship with the outer world than some of the regulations of this establishment. For instance, I have before me a standing resolution of the trustees, dated December the 6th, 1803, to the effect ‘ That, in future, if the parent or parents, or any relation or acquaintance of, or belonging to any of the children in Mr. Raine's asylum, stop to talk with any of them going to or from church, or churchyard, that the child or children so spoken unto shall be deprived of the holiday next ensuing; and if repeated shall be liable to censure or expulsion, as the trustees shall think proper; and that this resolution be printed and delivered to the parents or friends of the children on their admission into the Asylum.'

This example will suffice to show that we need some reformation, and I am glad that the trustees have taken the bull by the horns, and put themselves into communication with the Endowed Schools Commissioners. Sooner or later 'Raine's Charities' must have been overhauled, and it is better to court reformation than to wait for changes which might be more radically severe than the governing body would relish.

It would hardly interest my readers if I were to go into the projects of the trustees for the better application of the charity at their disposal than is possible under the existing rules. We hope to see divers desirable educational improvements effected in the direct instruction of the children, and some better ordering of the other provisions made for them under Mr. Raine's will. The disposal of the marriage portion has, *c. g.*, been attended with some very unpleasant circumstances even during the short time I have been associated with St. George's; and in the retention of this custom great care will be needed to make it more wholesome in its operation. Out of the three or four who have drawn the prize since I have been here, two have been incapacitated for receiving it through double dealing on the part of either the girls or their suitors. One girl, well knowing that both she and her man were bound to be members of the Episcopal Church of England, concealed the fact that they were both strong Nonconformists till the marriage itself was coming on, and it appeared that they were seeking the money under false pretences. The girl had drawn the prize. Another, who also had drawn the £100 prize, presented as her future husband a man who failed hopelessly to fulfil the ordinary conditions of the trustees. On his finding that she could not receive the marriage portion, he jilted her; and she brought an action for breach of promise of marriage against him. There was another matrimonial collapse, of which I forget the particulars, about the time that I came to St. George's. In short, the whole business wants the revision which the trustees now desire. It may well be questioned whether large powers should not be given to them in respect to the application of the money devoted to the provision of the marriage portion, so that the spirit of the Founder's intentions should be carried out, and deserving girls be settled in marriage without the drawbacks now attendant on the process. For instance, I think myself that the drawing of lots for the £100, though it certainly provides an easy way of settlement among a number of claimants, is in some respects objectionable. Mr. Raine, who seems to have been specially considerate and self-denying, sets forth in his will that in order to provide for his nephews as well as for the girls of the asylum, he had kept himself unmarried, and 'he doubted not but that his said nephews would cheerfully' acquiesce in his setting aside a part of his substance for the perpetual provision of the marriage portions 'if his nephews had seen, as he had, six poor innocent maids come trembling to draw the prize, and the fortunate maid that got it burst out into tears with excess of joy.' Yes. But how about the rest? The worthy Mr. Raine does not tell us of the bitter disappointment of the *five* 'poor innocent maids,' who had of course all provided themselves with suitors, and came 'trembling' in hope of being soon settled comfortably in life, but drew blanks.

When I had been some time at St. George's, the trustees were pleased to do me the honour of electing me as their chairman, and one of the duties I had soon to perform was to preside over this lottery, and, according to custom, deliver two addresses, one to the successful and the other to the unsuccessful; and in speaking to the latter I could not mingle my consolations with any warm defence of a process which keeps a girl in unwholesome suspense at a crisis in her life when mere 'luck' ought not to affect her prospects. Though the 'drawing' is conducted elaborately and seriously, the marriage of the unsuccessful is at least deferred, and the whole thing resolves itself into something very like the 'tossing up' for a husband.

However, the prize, and the excitement naturally attending the getting of it, has of course made the attendant ceremonies so conspicuously popular in the parish that the asylum is commonly known as the 'Hundred Pound' School, and we have a large gathering to see the 'poor innocent maids' dip their hands into the vessel that holds the tickets. But, with all respect for the memory of Mr. Raine, I doubt if this generosity of his, as now applied, promotes real thrift and righteous love. I have already stated that there have been sad cases of attempted imposture during the very short time that I have known anything about the matter, and while the settling of good girls in desirable marriages may well be an object in which the trustees should concern themselves, I hope that the chance elements in the business will be modified or corrected in the new scheme which they have applied for. The marriages themselves, with their attendant bell-ringing, sermon, and publicity, the ceremonious presentation of the marriage portion, the popular processions through the parish, and the stated entertainments at the asylum, might all be retained without a process which conspicuously supports the assertion of those who say that marriage is a lottery.

It would take me too long, and I should become too statistical, if I were to attempt to enter upon the condition of education generally in the East of London. Many, though, would be pleased to learn, as they might, that it can show national schools which for efficiency and self-support, set an example to the metropolis. In these, however, the fees are too high for the poorest class, whose schools have been to a great extent created and kept alive by strong public appeals on the part of their promoters. I venture to think that the School Board must eventually provide for the education of these 'masses' throughout London. It is not well that this should be done by the sheer importunity of their school managers. Indeed, one of the unfortunate accompaniments or results of strenuous efforts to provide and maintain schools by begging of the richer part of the metropolis and the country, has been seen in the temptation laid upon their promoters to describe the people as worse than they were. Some earnest well-wishers of the poor, who have devoted themselves with energy to hard work among large masses of neglected people, naturally anxious to make out as good a case as possible in pleading for help, especially in the establishment of schools, have unwittingly brought undue discredit upon whole districts by setting forth their condition in the darkest colours. Thus the best intentions have resulted in the creation of an evil impression about the condition of the East of London, which is, to say the least of it, in many respects exaggerated and injurious, and which is slow to pass away. I am persuaded that some zealous promoters of educational as well as other charitable work in this part of the metropolis have done more harm by their pictures of assumed eastern depravity than good with the money collected from the public by means of harrowing appeals.

The application of the voluntary principle, shrewdly strained in the laudable struggle to provide and maintain schools for those who are too poor to provide and maintain them themselves, has gradually resulted in the 'Mendicant System,' which, while it has characterized the educational work of the metropolis, has engendered or encouraged a habit of begging, from which few of us parsons are free. I do not think that we deserve the blame which is sometimes freely laid upon us, for many have begged sorely against the grain, with sheer desire to better the condition of those in whom we are most immediately concerned. Still it must, I suppose, be admitted that the whole pastoral economy of London, including the north, south, and west, as well as east, is penetrated and tainted with the spirit of mendicancy, which has tended to demoralise instead of elevate those amongst whom it has worked, parsons included.

But a better day is dawning. The London School Board releases those of us clergy who would thus be released from the suppliant attitude we have been compelled to take in order to provide primary education for the people; the Charity Organization Society supplies us with some escape from small pottering habits of philanthropy which mostly fail in their good purpose: the growing conviction that improved dwellings can be provided on commercial rather than charitable principles for the working classes opens an enormous prospect of social and moral improvement amongst those who need it most; and the Charity Commissioners—under whatever name they work—help forward the wise application of antiquated and hide-bound endowments.

SOME notice of these may properly follow the few remarks which I have made about education, for the object of the best of these institutions is not only to provide shelter for sailors, and to draw them from evil ways, but to educate them in habits of thrift, and to instruct them in seamanship and navigation.

I have noticed the sore temptations to which, when on shore, they are exposed in these parts, and from which, less than fifty years ago, they had virtually no escape, being left to every kind of evil influence and unfair treatment that the debased and greedy were only too eager to ply them with. The most practised and cunning parasites were always ready to pounce upon poor Jack and wheedle the hard-earned coin out of his pocket directly he touched ground. I am afraid that the Ratcliff Highway and its immediate tributaries provided an army of crimps and dissolute tempters as experienced and deadly as could well be found.

In the last half century, however, a great change has been brought about. Not only are improved facilities afforded for the safe custody of a sailor's wages, or the transmission of them to his family, but means are provided for his protection while on shore. There are divers institutes and associations for the benefit of seamen, but there is one in this immediate neighbourhood so good in its object, and, it would seem, so wisely conducted, that my readers will, I am sure, be interested in hearing something about it.

The 'Sailors' Home' in Dock Street was instituted in 1830, opened in 1835, and enlarged in 1863. It is now capable of sheltering 500 men, and provides them, by means of stores under its roof, with everything a sailor is likely to want, at a fair price. On entering the building by the Dock Street entrance it is obvious at once that the place is well appreciated by those for whom it is built, for that kind of management is adopted which does not deter by its primness men who are necessarily penetrated with some sort of holyday feeling, and are conscious of money in their pockets. Numbers of tanned and hearty-looking seamen are to be seen lounging about at their ease. If they want refreshment they can get it at a handy bar inside the house, without the risk of finding a crimp at their elbows; and close by is a busy bank, where they can lay by what they do not immediately want of their wages. It struck me when I lately visited the place that the bank was being more used than the bar.

The whole place smacks of the sea. A large dial placed on the wall of the entrance is so sensitively connected with a wind vane on the roof that the least change in the successive puffs of a breeze betrays itself conspicuously. The hand on the plate wavers so constantly that I am sure I know people who would be made sea sick by watching it. There is, of course, to be found here the very best meteorological advice which the barometer is capable of giving, and while charts and maps are not forgotten, the most prominent ornaments in the place consist of elaborately rigged and equipped models of ships.

The building is large. In the basement are

the kitchen, store-rooms, larder, butcher's shop,
laundry, &c., &c. Here also is placed the navigation school, which has done good service, many
having by its means passed their examinations for
the posts of second and chief mates, as well as for
those of masters. In one part of the basement
are situated the bath-rooms and barber's shop;
and a skittle alley is not forgotten. But this last
is, I am told, not much used, probably because
it needs a level floor, which sailors seldom
have. The two next floors are occupied by the
dining-hall, library, reading-room, clothing department, bank, bar, smoking-rooms, &c., with various
other offices, and a Mission Hall. There are daily
morning and evening prayers, with other frequent
services in this last, which are occasionally attended
by a good many men; but the managers of the
institution, while they openly take Godliness as
the basis and motive of their work, are wisely
careful not to press its inmates with too importunate invitations to take part in religious worship,
knowing that undue pressure sometimes provokes
a reaction. Much good seems to have been done
in connection with this Mission Hall and its.

missionary. The second and third floors are wholly devoted to sleeping berths, with lavatories attached. There are some 500 of these cabins, each of which is about 8 feet long by 5 feet wide, and suitably furnished. In every cabin, moreover, there is a copy of the Holy Scriptures.

It would, I think, be difficult to find any work which more directly met the needs of a neighbourhood and gave more encouragement to a philanthropist than the Sailors' Home. For the best of it is that the institution has become almost entirely self-supporting, and the directors, in their last annual report, state that they 'now look forward hopefully to the time when the Home will no longer stand in need of pecuniary aid from the public.' The balance sheet appended to the report fully justifies this hope, for while the income of the institution is set down as £12,232 16s. 0d., £11,101 10s. 11d. is received from the sailors who make use of it. Of the difference between these sums, only the modest sum of £167 6s. 0d. arises from donations and subscriptions, and £219 19s. from legacies. These together make £387 5s. Now since in the account of the expenditure a balance is reported of £377 4s. 9d., after the investment in stock of £1,400 0s. 0d., it does not require much knowledge of arithmetic to enable the reader to perceive that this wholesome Sailors' Home is fairly afloat. The large number of 11,305 seamen have been lodged and boarded here during the year, and their use of the Bank in the establishment has been most encouraging. Of course the greatest pains are taken to assist them and their friends with postal facilities, and information about absent relations, and communications are kept up with Sailors' Homes elsewhere in different parts of the world. A visit to this in Dock Street would repay those of my readers who like to see a good work done well, and some might be tempted to aid the good cause to which it is devoted, not by mere subscriptions, but by helping forward elsewhere some such institution as really contains within it the seeds of self-support. One important feature of Sailors' Homes, which those who would support them should bear in mind, is, that they are 'Homes,' *i. e.*, places in which the sailor, during his time on shore, is lodged and boarded. This is the speciality of the place of which I have spoken ; and considering the peculiar situation of the class it is sought to benefit, I doubt whether any institution which does not make this the chief phase of its work is likely to do much good. Jack does not want merely to be talked to, but to have some comfortable and respectable roof under which to live, and some trustworthy resident friend to take care of his money or help him to lay it out to the best advantage till he goes to sea again.

IT was my purpose in writing this little book to devote separate chapters to the moral, social, religious, and physical condition of the people in the East of London, comparing it where I could with the impressions I had received in the course of my ministerial work in the West. But I found, as I might have seen beforehand, that it was impossible to disentangle the results of such observation as I could make so as to present them separately. I have therefore given up the attempt to classify the notes I had made about these phases of life, and shall take them as they come. That is, indeed, the order in which they naturally arrive in actual experience. Physical, moral, and religious influences are too intimately involved and intertwined to permit their formal separation.

The statistics which give some account of the morality of a district as tested by the proportion of drinking-houses to the population in the various divisions of the metropolis, would seem to show that in the Tower Hamlets, comprising Bethnal Green, St. George's in the East, and such parishes as contain a very large proportion of poor, the number of persons to every drinking-shop is greater than in Westminster—I quote extracts published in the *Times* from a Parliamentary Return for the year ending March 31, 1875—and that thus there is more drinking in the latter than in the former part of London. But there is not much to choose in this respect among the Metropolitan Boroughs. I mention the matter only to remark that we do not seem to be worse than our neighbours, considering the large preponderance of the labouring class amongst us. In respect to other kinds of intemperance, there are, of course, exhibitions of gross profligacy in all sea-ports, especially in the neighbourhood of docks, wherever they may be found; and as London is, I suppose, the largest sea-port in the world, and as moreover the London Docks are mainly situated in the parish of St. George's in the East, we ought to have our full share of grievous and open debauchery. And we have. It is gratifying, however, to know that examples of steady Christian life are conspicuous in many who live in those of our streets which are counted as least reputable by the public.

Ratcliff Highway, our chief thoroughfare, has got a bad name. Years ago, when most of the coal used in London was brought by sea, and the 'Pool' was crowded with colliers, the riot and indecency of the Highway was excessively shocking. I have heard descriptions of the scenes habitually witnessed there which I could hardly set down on paper. Now, though we have a crowd of ships in our Docks, a large proportion of which are 'ocean-going,' the 'Pool' is comparatively bare of colliers, the 'forest of masts' below London Bridge has been felled, and the troops of coal-grimed satyrs who disported themselves in their hours of relaxation along its banks have mostly disappeared. The result has been a great diminution in the retail trade of the Highway, and also in the profuse debauchery which accompanied it. Moreover, the provision of Sailors' Homes, and the facilities afforded for sending their money to their families, has very much checked riotous local expenditure.

The once famous, or infamous, Highway is very unlike what I am told it was. Still it is, at times, bad enough in all conscience. I say ' at times,' for it often is so quiet that friends of mine, ignorant of the East of London, have been almost unwilling to believe me when, after walking down it for some distance, I have said, ' This is the Ratcliff Highway.'

Occasionally, however, this quiet is disturbed, for this street is still the chief promenade of sailors, from all nations, ashore for a few hours' dissipation. And yet I was surprised the other day at trying to reckon up the number of regular attendants at our church, and Sunday-school teachers, who reside there. The respectable and dissolute strata of society in the Highway and its immediate affluents keep themselves strictly apart. Not that I have observed any severity or bitterness of Pharisaic judgment in those who live decently. On the contrary, it is from several steady communicants that I have heard the kindest utterances of extenuation for the most grossly degraded. These last, moreover, are civil enough to those who leave them alone, and they never by word or gesture offer any offence to the great bulk of reputable residents or wayfarers. I can scarcely say the same of some places in the West which are highly esteemed in society.

But hitherto, at St. George's, I have never been the subject of any remark or incivility by harlots or their dissolute companions. It is curious, moreover, that these fallen women have their phase of honest industry. I have frequently noticed that as they lounge about the corners of the streets they are engaged in knitting. What they knit, and how they dispose of their knitted wares, I have been at a loss to perceive or discover, but they mostly knit, and divers of them carry babies. I have been also told by those who know the neighbourhood and its ways better than myself that there is an illegitimate sort of faithfulness recognised between many individuals among them and the particular sailors with whom they are associated. Indeed I venture to say that before God I think the harlotry of the Haymarket is radically worse than that of the Ratcliff Highway. There is this difference, that in the latter thoroughfare the dress of the degraded is outrageously flaring, and in the other studiously fashionable. With us, white muslin gowns and red boots are supposed to be attractive. But the poor sailors are chiefly the prey that is sought. And—I hardly know how to put it politely, though the truth ought to be noticed—there is more excuse for intemperance in men who have been afloat for months, and who pursue their pleasures coarsely, than for the cultivated and continuous sensuality of such as risk their health and waste their substance in the riotous living that characterizes the resorts and centres of profligacy in the West. No doubt the Eastern dissoluteness of which I speak is more painfully and conspicuously repulsive, and it is sometimes accompanied by fights among the women themselves which are frightfully personal and persistent, but, considered fairly, the West has less to be said in palliation of it.

These fights between women are indeed among the most painfully distressing phases of unright-eousness that a clergyman ever comes across. I have stopped several (not at St. George's), though in almost terror of my life, for attendant sons of Belial are likely to interfere. I remember once intervening in a hideous duel between two viragos, whose rage was inexpressible. But the unexpected interference of a parson, who held the combatants asunder at arm's length, had an influence which was well-nigh grotesque. It certainly answered. But I hope I may never have to try it again.

Sometimes a comical result follows intervention when fair play is not being duly observed. One evening I found a big boy mercilessly thrashing a little one in the street. I intervened, laying hold of the bully. Seeing him thus hampered, the little fellow hit him so straight a blow from the shoulder in the eye that I let my man go, half blinded by the prompt use of the opportunity for a Nemesis, which the defendant had perceived and accepted.

Altogether, judging of the comparative immorality and sin of any sort presented in poor or wealthy localities, it must be remembered that the 'Street' comes to be a prominent meeting-place and scene of entertainment among such of the 'poor' as live bad lives. No doubt the parlours of some public-houses, especially those low-browed, dingy beershops, which have no great crowd outside, are scenes of sad social mischief. Indeed the house which has a brilliant gas-lit front and a large 'bar' is frequently the best conducted, for the poor tattered sots who hang about outside do so because they are not allowed lodgment within. The bulk of their customers come and go quickly, and they are largely used by such as send to them for their dinner or supper beer, being to a great extent the cellars of their district. They do not rely upon that stifling, drunken session which disgraces those of less pretension. Indeed the street is in divers instances the chief place of assembly and scene of offence with many who least respect themselves among the working classes. Domestic differences, social disputes, and impure overtures are public. When a man or woman exceeds the license of the most tolerant publican, the offender is thrust out of doors. Now if all the irregularities, excesses, and delinquencies of the rich were displayed in the roadway, the respective states of morality in low and high places could be more fairly compared.

No doubt there is a refinement of transgression which indicates at least an emancipation from the more brutal and degrading forms of evil, but sin is sin, whether it be coarse or refined. Evil passions are evil, whether those who suffer from them are well or badly dressed and housed. What might be termed the private ill-conduct of a poor man is never hidden, and cannot be indulged in without the cognisance of his friends and acquaintances. The son of the household in the family of an artisan who sows his wild oats mostly sows them under the nose of his parents ; whilst in other classes they frequently do not even hear of the youthful 'indiscretions,' as they are called, of which he may be guilty. These domestic troubles are all patent or published in the society of the working classes ; their conditions of life render privacy almost impossible.

In fact among the poor there are no skeletons in 'cupboards.' However painfully they expose family affairs, they are never hidden ; and though there is undoubtedly some advantage in the concealment of offences and defects, it may be questioned whether, in the sight of God, the frailties and offences of the 'poor' are not often far too severely judged by those whose faults are or have become more refined, and who are, in a great measure, enabled to screen them from public observation.

As to the physical condition of the working-classes in the East, or at least that part of the East in which I live, compared with that I know most of in the West, I might fill many pages with interesting statistics; but I will not weary my readers with them.   I must however quote two or three facts from the last printed reports of our Medical Officer of Health, which may indicate the state of our affairs in this respect.   The annual birth-rate of St. George's for the last ten years has averaged 40 for every 1,000 of its population.   That of the whole of London has been for the same period, ten years, 37 per 1,000.   Thus there seems to be a reserve of productive power in the place. But through carelessness, I believe, as much as evil sanitary condition, our death-rate is swelled by the large proportion of children who die.   Out of our total deaths in the last published report during twelve months, nearly one-half were infants under the age of five years.   Our Medical Officer of Health, Dr. Rygate, remarks: 'It is true that our parish very greatly supplies the labour-market with many in those periods of life which show the lowest mortality, and these being drafted off, we are left with the very young and very old.' But the large proportion of deaths among the very young indicates great carelessness rather than a radically bad state of the conditions of life, for the tabular statement of deaths for the last ten years from fever, smallpox, measles, scarlet fever, and diphtheria, diarrhœa, and whooping-cough, gives a marked decrease in the general total, and in every affection, save whooping-cough and diarrhœa, the maladies from which ill-nursed infants mostly die. Again, of the 98 cases of deaths from diarrhœa which appear in the last annual report of our Medical Officer of Health, 65 occurred in infants under 1 year of age. And he has been able to find out that as many as 36 of these infants were being brought up ' by hand.' He remarks, moreover: ' How much of this mortality is prevented at the West-end, and wealthier parts of London, by wet-nursing ? ' And he adds : ' How frequently do I find upon enquiry that our parish is the source of these fostermothers, their own children remaining here to be brought up by hand or the bottle, a stereotyped, but very indefinite phrase.'

Thus, in regard to some phases of our physical condition, it would seem that the things which should have been for our wealth are unto us an occasion of falling.

Our present exemption from small-pox is very gratifying. In the last published annual report only one death is recorded to have resulted from it in a population of about 50,000, and on enquiry our medical officer found that this had not been correctly registered. The same report gives only ten deaths from fever as having occurred during the preceding twelve months. It is true that in no year has so favourable a condition of things existed. In one month, however, an outbreak occurred in a court, chiefly among children, and the cases were removed. 'Three of the dwellings were closed as unfit for habitation until properly cleansed and disinfected. Another was well fumigated and disinfected, the inmates leaving their home for a time for the purpose.'

On the whole the sanitary condition of our parish is not such as many heedlessly think, who look on the East of London as a region of perpetual distress or depression. We have, indeed, very much need of improvement; for though, as I have already remarked, the 'poor' have certainly more room with us than in the central and west-central parts of London, they live far too closely and carelessly for anything like the exercise of proper caution when a disease, such as scarlet-fever, is epidemic. When an infectious disorder makes its appearance I often wonder how any one escapes. Our medical and sanitary officers do what they can, as in other poor localities in London, and yet the intercourse among the poor is so constant and unrestricted that, by all the laws of contagion, every accessible person ought, it would seem, to suffer. There are, however, mysteries involved in the history of epidemics which have not been, and cannot perhaps be, explained. For instance, in the last visit of scarlet-fever to London we had some share, when, all at once, the matter which conveyed the disease seemed to lose its virulence. The plague came and went; and that is pretty nearly all that can be said about it. Any one who knows how inefficiently the directions given by medical officers and others to the poor are carried out, even under the best supervision that has yet been exercised in London, must allow that the disappearance of scarlet-fever from a district is but slightly due to scientific or sanitary proceedings adopted when the plague has made its appearance. They may check its progress or alleviate its intensity in some instances, but, considering the subtlety with which it is propagated, it cannot account for the rapid subsidence of the disease. It is otherwise with cholera, since, through the evidence afforded by the famous Broad Street pump, in the midst of my old district of St. Luke's, the chief vehicle of the latter has been proved to be water ; and in the case of small-pox, vaccination provides a shield of influence which it would be well for those who question it to consider the results of, in the medical statistics in reference to this matter which have been published.

I was exceedingly interested and concerned in the treatment of cholera when it visited London in 1866. Everyone who knows anything of the matter has heard of the terrible outbreak of this disease in St. Luke's, Berwick Street, in 1854. I am afraid to say how many hundreds died in a few days within a bow-shot of the church. Thus the appearance of cholera in London had a specially significant sentiment attached to it by ourselves, though in reality the chief cause of the mischief it did there had been discovered and corrected.

Still there was need of great circumspection and care. And I mention what we did to show how much can be done by prompt parochial combination and a wholesome fear of trusting too much to official ability and zeal. The leading residents met together in one of the rooms under the church. We divided the parish into manageable districts, and, acting in concert with the local sanitary authorities, in a few days inspected every drain, cistern, and ash-pit in the place, besides putting, as far as we could, all on their guard, without alarming them. I was personally aided in the part I took in the matter by my dear friend the late Dr. Anstie, who was always ready as a champion to fight with disease, dirt, and disorder of any and every kind. We had several cases of cholera. Two occurred in one house, brought, I think, from Bow. And how well I recollect seeing the clothes, bedding, &c., of the sufferers burnt myself. Each case was beaten out as if it were a flake of fire on thatch, and we had no 'outbreak' of the malady. Altogether it was a very interesting period of watchfulness and sanitary effort. Indeed the thorough, though unauthorised, inspection we made of the dwellings in the district resulted in such a wholesale and detailed scrubbing, whitewashing, and mending of drains, traps, &c., that the general health of the neighbourhood was thereby sensibly improved. I had ever so much fault found with me afterwards for interference in some cherished cases of domestic dirtiness, for I had ventured to arm our visitors with an official-looking printed paper directing such and such enquiries to be made and defects remedied. People submitted to our intrusion without suspecting that we had no authority whatever for what we did. Many, indeed, thanked us, but some did not find out our unofficial character till it was too late.

Moreover the revelation made, though I say it myself, by amateur investigation in the case of a late visit of small-pox to St. James's, Westminster, was such that I am constrained to set it down. At St. Luke's we took steps to see that children were vaccinated, and quite an eagerness to be 'done' was set up in the school when I had my own arm operated upon, and sat in the boys' room with my coat off and shirt sleeve rolled up. Several little folk who had been overlooked came afterwards to be vaccinated, with almost a complaint that they had missed their share in the general treatment.

The disinfection of clothes, &c., was, of course, an important matter, and I was astonished when in the course of my enquiries I discovered that no adequate provision existed for it. I came across a heap of infected bedding belonging to some servants who had had small-pox in one of the clubs in Pall Mall. Pursuing this, I found that the only means for its disinfection appeared in an iron gas-heated box about five feet long by two wide and two deep, which had been used to kill vermin in the clothes of 'casuals' at the workhouse. This implement or vessel was obviously unfit for the disinfection of bedding used in small-pox cases. It was much too small, and could not be sufficiently heated. Moreover the bedding, &c., was brought in a wooden truck, and after being little more than warmed was sent back in the same vehicle. I must say that though the members of the Vestry who were concerned in the sanitary matters of the parish did not seem at first inclined to believe my statements, they accompanied me to the 'Stone-yard,' where this futile iron box stood, and allowed me to measure it with a two-foot rule in their presence. The result was eventually the provision of a suitable hot disinfecting chamber and furnace for the parish. I may add that in one place in London (not St. George's) where I was having a sanitary hunt I was assured that infected bedding had been sent to be baked in the oven of a baker's shop, which is not a nice mode of disinfection to think of, however efficacious it may have been. I only wish that any man, though without official authority, who suspects any defects in the sanitary machinery of his parish would be content with nothing less than an importunate personal investigation of it. I am sure that he would receive the thanks of any permanent official who was worth his salt.

But I must return to St. George's in the East. We still suffer from the want of enforcement of some sanitary laws. We have as yet no proper arrangements for the disinfection of clothes and bedding, though we have talked about them. I would also instance smoke. It is true that fewer blacks settle on the papers on my study-table here than when I lived in Duchess Street. This is partly accounted for by the fact that mine is a detached house, and its windows do not immediately invite the smuts from a next-door chimney. But our lesser amount of blacks, which of course are most numerous where fires are most used, may be partly accounted for thus. The east wind is the coldest in London, and thus leads to the largest consumption of coal. And when the wind is in the east all our smuts go westward. On dark, cold winter days I have been much struck with the growing clearness or lessening thickness of the atmosphere, if I happened to move from the west to the east.

The great body of smoke in London comes, I imagine, from private houses, and can hardly be hindered; but that which arises from factory chimneys is capable of being at least lessened. And I do not see why the furnace of everybody's lungs should be compelled to consume the manufacturer's smoke. Chiefly around London there are hundreds of huge brick and mortar masts, from many of which long black banners stream day and night.   Any man might, of course, inform against his smoky neighbour, but this is a disagreeable procedure, and one which, as a parson, I have not hitherto had moral courage enough to adopt.   The provisions of the Smoke-Consuming Act are, however, not now enforced with half the vigilance which might be exercised even under existing powers.   This neglect is the less excusable, inasmuch as the nuisance I complain of is grossly obvious; and thus those who should protect us have no difficulty whatever in obtaining evidence of the offence.   There is the smoking chimney, and the imperfect furnace is sure to be found at the base of it.   We Londoners sorely want some official in the shape of a Public Prosecutor, who will compel the proper construction of furnaces, and relieve individuals and local corporations from the invidious task of summoning a next-door neighbour or large ratepayer before the magistrate for what is really an offence to the community at large.   As it is, each district suffers from the smoke of the next. If any reader has a lofty 'smoker' next door, his smuts, set flying 200 feet up in the air, pitch a mile away, while those which settle on his own door-step come mostly from a distant stranger. At St. George's whatever factory blacks we get during an east wind arrive chiefly from the neighbourhood of Bow, while a west wind brings us the smoke of ten thousand domestic chimneys, from Notting Hill to Whitechapel. But on the whole our sky is cleaner, or at least less dirty, than in the centre of London. I recollect, moreover, that on the occasion of the famous fogs in the winter of 1873 it was remarked in the papers that the plague was least in the neighbourhood of Wapping. Here, though, a fog is especially disastrous, since the edges of the quays which line the Docks are unguarded, and we had many cases of persons stepping over the edge and being drowned. As well as I recollect, some thirty persons thus lost their lives during the fog I refer to, in and about the Docks, and in one or two instances carts or waggons were fairly driven into the water from the inability of the driver, and one would suppose also of the horse, to perceive the stone rim which marked the boundary of safety.

The rough work of our neighbourhood results, I fear, in an excessive share of accidents, but some of the escapes are surprising. One day this year a

little boy fell fifty-two feet down a shaft connected
with the tunnel under the London Docks, and
escaped unhurt and without loss of consciousness.
The accident, moreover, had its grotesque phase.
A man working near the bottom of the shaft took
the lad for a log, and shoved him away with his
foot. Becoming aware of his mistake by the crying
out of the supposed log at being kicked, he looked
up the shaft and cried out, 'What did you "chuck"
this boy down here for?' Eventually they pulled
him out, as I said, none the worse for his tremendous
tumble.

I often wonder how the big ships which crowd
the Docks are got in and out of their stations without more damage to themselves and those who have
to guide them. But the men who manage these
matters, and who are experts, will bring a huge
vessel, some 300 feet long, into its place as neatly
as if it were a wheelbarrow, and seemingly
without scratching its paint. There is indeed a
nicety and gentleness in the right performance of
the roughest and heaviest work which is nowhere
better seen than in the skill with which the
ponderous and unwieldy hulls of ships are moved

about in a crowded dock. They have so long been driven of fierce winds, or urged at top speed with the screw from the utmost parts of the earth, that the transition in their movement to the cautious snail's pace with which they slide into their nooks, side by side, till they stop with their noses over the quay, seems almost to indicate intelligence on their part. They seem to smell their way in circumspectly, as if well knowing that a body representing, say, two thousand tons, held in a thin skin, must be careful how it touches the hard stone edge of the dock side.

But this is a divergence from the proper subject of this chapter, though it be suggested by some thoughts about the weighty character of the work in which many of our people are engaged. They have rough toil, and some of them are rough enough to look at, in all conscience. But there is an individuality in the roughness of the most laborious in these parts; and although of course we have a share of those who go by the name of ' roughs,' and some of them are strikingly the reverse of smooth, I seem to miss that peculiar form of unattached vagabondism which elsewhere slouches about the skirts of luxurious life, and which any gentleman reining in his horse almost anywhere about the West End of London is sure to see a specimen of present itself, as suddenly as if it had sprung out of the ground, to touch its battered hat and offer to hold his steed.   While I think of it, I cannot recall ever having seen a gentleman on horseback in St. George's.   And I doubt whether we have any appreciable proportion of that seedy servile race which hangs about the West.   True, we have some courts, fancied by thieves, though I believe that their evil business lies chiefly elsewhere ; and we have quite our share of so-called men who beat their wives, and whose exhibition of rough anger is less distressing when they ' punch ' each other's heads.   One fancies it is possible to detect the operation of a rude sort of Nemesis when two of these bullies come to blows. The feeling themselves of a rough and heavy hand, which is sometimes raised against a woman, must involve a wholesomely suggestive sensation when it falls on a man's own pate.

As to the great bulk of ' poor ' people inhabiting our streets, I can honestly say that they are very civil in respect to their reception of any pastoral visits. Knowing as I do something of those various parts of London which are most crowded, and having paid, in my time, literally thousands upon thousands of visits in all kinds of places where the poor chiefly congregate, I am especially struck with the civility, not servility, of the working people in these parts. There is little touching of hats, and curtseying, but I find a frankness and pleasantness of manner among them which is exceedingly wholesome. And many of their houses are clean and well kept. Even in courts of worst repute none of us have ever met with any rudeness, and some of the places which ought by all their associations to be dens of disorder exhibit a few exceptionally remarkable phases of neatness. I remember especially the home or lodging of a dying harlot, whom one of my colleagues was asked to visit. One morning I went with him to see her, and found her just dead. The room in which she died, and the sheets in which she lay, showed considerable respect for external cleanliness. Divers of loose characters were hanging about, and took kindly a few words of truth.

This was in a notorious, I might say infamous court. It had furnished Dickens with a scene. The readers of 'Edwin Drood' may recollect the spot to which Jasper betook himself for his opium smokes. This was the place. The old crone who received him, well-known as 'Lascar Sal,' lives, or lived till quite lately, in a court just beyond the end of our churchyard. And I know the 'John Chinaman' of whom she was jealous as a rival in her deadly trade. He had a ground floor in the same court, and a friend of mine who came to prowl about St. George's in the East could not complete his experience without going in to have a few whiffs at the opium pipe in his den. But in this court of evil fame we have been ever welcome when paying a kindly visit or attending the sick. It must, however, before very long, be pulled down, being in a grievously dilapidated state, and having some of its houses already shut up. Indeed it borders on the great chasm made through the parish by the construction of the East London Railway. More of this presently.

I now merely remark, that the affronts or insults which a visitor is assumed to be exposed to in the worst courts exist only in the imagination of those who know nothing about the matter, or they are invited by the visitor himself. If he sniffs about censoriously, and asks impertinent questions, or gives himself airs in any way, he is likely to meet with a rebuff which the offended party does not know how to convey in the shape of polished sarcasm.

As a rule, all over the world, in its ugliest corners, if you are civil to people they will be civil to you. And the most curious phases of social interest will sometimes turn up in the worst slums. I remember once being much interested in a specially unpleasant young blackguard whom I wanted to save. It happened while I was at St. Luke's, Berwick Street. This particular vagabond, poor fellow, had been ill brought up, and had had a bad example set him at home. I recollect that his mother had once to go to gaol for biting a neighbour's nose off. She was thus obviously a very ill-conditioned parent, and her son was a bad boy. Somehow I came to be especially interested in trying to draw him from the error of his ways ; but I lost sight of him for a long time, till one rainy day, as I was getting into a cab in Oxford Street, my rascal presented himself to shut the door. 'William,' said I, 'where do you live now?' He told me, and I presently routed out the place. It was one of those low lodging-houses where the street-door stands always open, .and the walls of the passage are greasy with the slouching shoulders of many generations of lodgers and tramps. Ultimately I got my rascal into a home, in which he partly recovered himself, and whence he emigrated to Canada, where he did well. I had a magnificent letter from him not so very long ago. Meanwhile, to go back to the days before his emigration, I had occasion to visit his dirty lodging. At my last call there the landlord, a grimy harbourer of thieves, remarked quite seriously, 'I understand, sir, that you have placed William in an institution;' adding, 'I thought, sir, he was going to make himself respectable, as he had been and bought a pair of trousers. But about the institution, sir: I do trust it is conducted on Protestant principles.' He was obviously a strong anti-ritualist.

Some of these thieves are very soft and nervous.

I remember once finding a city missionary being evil entreated by a parcel of roughs. I went, of course, to his rescue, and incidentally laid hold of one of the offenders by the arm in the course of my expostulations. I suppose I griped him harder than I intended, for he wept. Great tears made clean tracks down his dirty cheeks. They cry readily, do these roughs. One day, at St. Luke's, a pupil-teacher at our girls' school came running and flustered to my house, saying that she had been garotted and robbed in such and such a court, though the robber had found but little in her pockets. This was too bad, for I had been very kind to the evil characters of the neighbourhood; so I asked her what the garotter was like, and, on her describing him, I felt sure I knew not only my man, but where he lived. He was but a lad. I popped on my hat, and, posting off to the Marl-borough Street Police-court, and stating my case, asked for three constables. I took them to a certain house, and setting one at the front and another at the back, put the third into the door, like a ferret into a rabbit-hole, telling him he would find the offender in the second-floor front room.

Sure enough he was there. We took him straight before the magistrate, and he got three months within an hour of the commission of his offence. A companion of his, who was in the room with him, a bigger lout, cried copiously at the possibility of his being taken also. But we had no case against him.

The strenuousness of the personal appeals to his Christianity and charity when a clergyman is compelled to hand any offender over to the law is remarkably touching. Some years ago, at St. Luke's, we were for a period plagued by Irish boys who found amusement in lounging into the corridor communicating with the church, and, when the evening congregation had assembled, pushing one of the folding doors open, and howling into the church. Of course this sudden salute made the worshippers jump, but was highly comical to the saluting party. I went intentionally late to church one Sunday evening, and just as I got to the door heard the howl delivered. It was immediately followed by a rush of the performers, their leader running plump into my arms. He was a very ill-conditioned looking fellow, worse than a mere boy 'on a lark,' and at the instance of one of our churchwardens, who gave the offender into custody at the police office, was locked up for the night. The congregation of Irish who awaited me when the evening service was over, and who besought me to let him go free, used none but theological arguments and appeals. I was more unchristian than cruel, though I was both, and the whole business was very discreditable to me, considering the sacred character of my office, &c., &c. So they pleaded. But I have found that if a clergyman has occasion to appeal to the current magisterial law in defence of things and persons under his charge, it is mistaken charity in him to melt under pathetic remonstrance. We were troubled with no more of these Irish overtures to our service. Nothing is however of its kind more destructive of his due influence than for the parson to be continually appealing to the policeman ; and, though the provocation be strong, he must not interfere with physical force himself. I never did but once. That was in a very offensive case of insult--not to me, but to a parcel of school-girls—and there was no time for expostulation. Having a handy cane,

I thrashed the offender soundly, and so scientifically that I don't think he could have sat down with any comfort for a fortnight. Meeting that afternoon one of the Marlborough Street police magistrates, with whom I was acquainted, I told him what I had done, and said that perhaps I should have to appear before him for an assault. 'No fear of that,' he replied, 'I only wish you would do it again.' However, we had no more of the nuisance in question.

I think the boys are more 'owdacious' in the central parts of London than in the East. But perhaps this impression comes from the fact that here they are not bottled up so tight, and therefore show less effervescence. There is much misapprehension about the London 'Arab,' as he is called. Many of the most unruly and troublesome boys whom I have known have not been outcasts, but the children of decent parents, and far more mischievous than wicked. Most of them are simply 'pickles,' and turn out much better than the sober elders whom they affront would expect. The really tainted class keep chiefly to themselves. We had a gang of these young criminals in our streets at St.

Luke's, and I have often thought how mistaken an estimate is sometimes formed of the street boy or gutter child by a mere superficial observer, who might have seen some scores of all sorts playing near our school, a few minutes before two, and confounded them, unjustly. They all seemed much alike, but when the school-bell rang the true arabs were eliminated. While the others poured into the building they were left in the street, and might then be perceived to have been intent on some chuck-farthing business amongst themselves. The two classes did not amalgamate, although they were necessarily more or less mixed up. The distinction became more apparent when we got a playground. The respectable boys within it made, I think, more noise, and were more boisterous in their play than the arabs. These last are slouching and sly rather than uproarious, and they mostly congregate at the corner of a street, because there they have additional facilities for the detection and avoidance of a policeman. I have often noticed how on his approach the majority of imps in full strenuous play have taken no notice of him, while a certain number in the crowd have slipped sullenly off. These were the arabs, not to be confounded with those who mostly have no place but the street in which to romp about, and who naturally, in order to be less interfered with, choose the debateable strip between the foot-path and the carriage-way, especially when marbles are ' in,' for their sports. But such as these by no means deserve the evil character associated in the minds of some with the term 'gutter' children. The kerbstone, moreover, offers a convenient seat for such of the little bodies with short legs as need one, and becomes quite a sofa-stall when Punch stops and opens his theatre. Strangely enough, however, I have not yet seen a Punch in that part of the East of London which I know best.

I have already noticed that I have found much less begging at St. George's than I found in St. James's, Westminster. Lately, moreover, there has been a decrease in the amount of out-door relief. The subject of Pauperism and the application of the Poor-laws is one which I cannot enter into so fully as I would in this little book. I must, however, admit that I am more and more impressed with the conviction that much social mischief has been done by a system of liberal out-door relief. It tends to lower wages, to encourage improvidence, and to further the neglect of parents by their children. The inquiries made by the Charity Organisation Society, of which we have now a branch at St. George's, have revealed many cases of imposition on the part of those in the receipt of money from the rates. In a place like London it is extremely difficult to get at the truth about the resources of those who apply for public aid. The cunning of the pauperised is sometimes almost incredible. At the same time, while fresh cases of applicants for out-door relief should be severely investigated, the promoters of reform in Poor-law administration might show more tenderness than they sometimes do in dealing with aged widows who have long been in the receipt of some weekly allowance. Eighteenpence or two shillings a week is a small sum, but it often makes a great difference in the condition of a poor old woman who dreads the House, and will somehow potter on with her petty gains in washing or cleaning for neighbours, if she can see her way to the rent of the little room where she keeps her 'bits of sticks.' To look at the question from the economical side—and this becomes an especially serious one in a district where there are many needy ratepayers—I believe that divers of the poorest single old women are kept going with a little weekly allowance who would cost more if they were driven into the House by its withdrawal. And surely there should be some commentary of kindness in the administration of the law by the corporate representative body of a parish. Poor-law Guardians have of course no business to indulge their private feelings of benevolence at the cost of their neighbours, but the exhibition of some tenderness may well be asked at the hands of those who supply the funds for parochial relief, especially while the process of reformation is going on. It is useless to plead with the old and infirm among the poor that they would be more 'comfortable' in the House. Comfort is not to be measured solely by a sound roof, a clean bed, and fixed rations. The bird in a cage is in some respects more comfortable than one in a bush, especially when the leaves are off and the berries all eaten. And a slave under a kind master escapes some of the inconveniences of personal responsibility ; but nevertheless liberty is sweet, and residence in the Workhouse is, after all, only a form of incarceration, though an inmate may discharge himself. He must while there be subject to regulations which are doubtlessly annoying to him, and wear something like a prisoner's dress. The separation, moreover, of old couples, who have long run their humble course and come down the hill together, cannot be thought of without a hope that arrangements may be made for them not to be parted till the Great Divider separates them. While a wholesome reform of this branch of parochial administration is needed, and improvements are made in it, which in the end will benefit the class who furnish paupers, the reformers must not be too 'doctrinaire.' It is better even to let some small abuses die out rather than summarily put them down. The feelings of the million, which surely should be consulted, are infinitely less hurt by severe caution in the entertainment of fresh applications for parochial relief than by sharply cutting off the small weekly allowances of old people, who cannot long continue to burden the rates, and many of whom would, in the ordinary course of things, have soon drifted into the Work-house or Infirmary. I will not, however, dwell on the large question of Parochial Relief, and the way in which this generation should face the problem of Pauperism left by mischievous legislation, which reaches far back into the past; but I think that, even in the interest of those who are most needy and improvident, the day in which out-door relief is, if not discontinued, at least very much reduced, will be seen by all to accompany a more wholesome state of affairs than has lately existed.

Meanwhile I do not think there has been sufficient recognition of the great trouble Guardians of the Poor have been at in the discharge of their duty. It is well for complaining Parishioners to point to defects in the administration of the law, but, I would ask some of them if they have taken pains to see it better administered ? Are no thanks due to those representatives of the ratepayers, to whom time is money, and who spend hours weekly in the adjudication of relief, being paid nothing for their pains ? Parochial corporations have often had but scant justice done to them, and though there are battles in most Vestries, which are signs of life, many who speak slightingly of them have little idea of the time and labour voluntary parochial officials spend in the administration of the affairs of a populous parish, and what an essential element they represent in English life. With us the Vestry is much more representative of the parish than I knew it to be in the West. Indeed East London is obviously much more really 'London' than those parts of the metropolis where a great bulk of the residents, and those often the wealthiest, are merely lodgers for a season, and take no interest whatever in the cares of self-government.

Our Vestry Hall, a handsome central edifice, admirably equipped. is much more plainly the focus of representative parochial management than similar buildings in some parts of the metropolis which are dwarfed by or lost in a crowd of mansions, whose inmates know little or nothing of the business of the Parish in which they live, and of the trouble in conducting it undergone by fellow parishioners less conspicuous in the eyes of the world than themselves.

THE colloquial form which I have allowed this book to assume encourages me, at the risk of being thought to take my readers too closely by the button, and talking too much about my own experience and opinions, to say something more of past efforts, and of our present plans and projects at St. George's.

I remarked at the first that if I ventured at all to respond to the proposal that I should write on these matters, I must necessarily be personal; and thus I must speak not only of what I have tried to do, but also of what I want to see done. This last, indeed, forms a prominent phase in the procedure of any man who is anywise interested in his calling. The course of a clergyman's work has been called 'a succession of experiments.' There is something depressing in this definition, and yet these attempts are not to be despised because they are transitory. By experiments we accumulate knowledge; but these pastoral efforts are, it is to be hoped, something more than experiments. Each has some distinct effect in stirring the stagnant air into which we are all apt to lapse. They are efforts, each attended at the time by some good to those whom they reach, and really, though perhaps almost imperceptibly, promoting radical corporate growth. The individual effort may seem to die down, but still it leaves a measure of healthy seed to spring up in the place of some social mischief, or to reappear in another shape. We walk by faith; we are saved by hope. Life is too dull to be lived without some project in view. And thus, though many may smile at the smallness of our schemes, I cannot speak about my work in the East and West of London without reference to what I have done, and failed to do, and also much which I yearn to see accomplished. Of course most clergymen have some enterprise in hand beyond the precise discharge of their most sacred duties. These come first; but they can hardly help being accompanied by some project for the material, social, and moral bettering of a class, a community, or a neighbourhood.

It will be perceived that in this little book I have not attempted, or even intended, to dwell on modes of strictly ministerial work, such as the visitation of the sick, management of Sunday-schools, Bible-classes, and methods of preaching. I have rather tried to set forth the state of things by which a clergyman finds himself surrounded, and his general relation to the people amongst whom he ministers, and in respect to whom his first, central, and last object is to awaken and help to guide the spirit of Godliness in the largest and deepest sense of the word. But no work of any kind is really worth doing except in a truly righteous spirit. However secular it may seem to be, it is mixed up with the working of the laws of God, and can be done aright only on the lines of the Great Worker. That which is good is of God, though it be but the sweetening of a drain ; and that which is anywise right has its inevitable relation to the Lord of Righteousness. Bearing, I trust, this in mind, I here speak mainly of those matters which some might think of mere secondary importance. It is well however to recollect that if the First Commandment tells of love to God, the

Second, which treats of love of our neighbour, is like unto it; and the ramifications of goodwill towards men are manifold and infinite, embracing the children that play in the market-place, and the largest principles of life that affect the well-being of a nation or a church.

In what remains to be said in these pages I seek to keep myself on the lines I have tried to follow; and in speaking of some trials I have had, or hopes and prospects which I now entertain, dwell on the collateral work of the minister, not despising little things which have come in my way whilst engaged in the stricter work of the ministry. Every clergyman knows how constantly he is required to see to matters which those amongst whom he serves rightly think to be such as he may well be expected to show an interest in. Thus a kindly feeling, which is of great price, may be kept up, without the sense of the duties of his sacred office being anywise dimmed or disregarded. Indeed it is to me one of the great charms of the Church of England, and one of the most wholesome signs of its life, that the man is not merged in the priest, but that he is expected by the people amongst whom he serves to be the minister of 'good,' and that 'good' involves far more than the round of those offices which are accounted to be directly sacred or religious, and embraces questions of social recreation and entertainment, as well as those connected with habits of providence, economy, and bodily health.

In these respects I have had some small successes. But it is curious to note how, occasionally, one idea takes a material shape with the least effort, while another hangs long and heavily in hand. I never did, in its way, a better stroke of secular parochial work than when I found myself, years ago, President of the St. Luke's Cricket Club, and with virtually no place to play in. So, believing in direct application to head-quarters, I sat down and wrote what I thought was a convincing letter to Lord John Manners, then in office. I asked him to appropriate to us a portion of the Regent's Park. To our great delight—and, I confess, my own surprise—I was almost immediately furnished with a document granting my request. We set off and pitched our wickets, to be suddenly descended upon by divers conscientious custodians of the Park, who, with proper official asperity, set about warning us off. Of course, under existing regulations, we were impertinent intruders. But the exhibition of our passport protected us. Really we were the bristle to the thread. The Government office was speedily besieged by cricket-clubs from all the contiguous parts of London ; and, permission having been once granted, a considerable portion of the park came eventually to be set aside for their play. I never pass those exclusive acres now without thinking of our first visit there, when we surprised the almost incredulous officials with the display of the written permission with which we had been so kindly furnished under the administration of Lord John Manners. This was a mere passing shot in the way of parochial schemes, but it had the ultimate effect of providing a large portion of London with a space in which to play as well as walk about.

Other and more important schemes were long in taking a practical shape. There was, *e.g.*, our St. Luke's Working Men's Club. We began, of course, with a public meeting, at which much enthusiasm was displayed, and then we passed, as is usual in such cases, into a very small party really prepared for business. I do not think there were above a dozen of us. Well, presently, two or three of them—working men—asked me whether I would apply to some of the potentates in St. James's for funds to set us up. But this I steadily refused to do, saying that unless they were prepared to try their own legs they had no right to expect to stand or walk. So we went on in a small room with a sanded floor, a few wooden chairs, a few papers, and a little band of members. Difficulties of all sorts arose, and the infant society nearly died of convulsions associated with teething.

I remember a very seriously propounded question about suspected clerical influence. Some thought, I suppose, that I had underhand schemes for committing the club to unfair clerical influences. However, to make a long story short, we survived. A gentleman lent us some money at 5 per cent. We stuck to the original principle of self-support, and when I visited the club some little time ago, in the twelfth or thirteenth year of its life, it numbered more than 300 paying members, and was conducted much on the principle of those in Pall-Mall. A committee was appointed by the members. Every candidate had to be proposed. His name was set forth along with his address, the name of his proposer, and his trade. This information was made public to the club, and men were then elected or rejected by the committee. The club bought its own liquors, and had its reading-room, billiard-room, and servants. There were two full-sized tables in the billiard-room, and these proved a lucrative source of income, the losers paying the club threepence for every game, fifty up. It had some educational features, the committee providing French and drawing-classes. Several changes were made in its management, as experience taught the managers. For instance, it was for some time found cheaper to send to an eating-house for food than to keep a cook. Now the cooking is done on the premises, as at the Athenæum or the Reform Clubs, though we have not had a Francatelli or a Soyer. I ceased to be a member of the committee long before I left St. Luke's, and saw little of the club; but once or twice I was asked to dinner there, and had a very good meal and a kindly welcome. Of course the club had its ups and downs, and on one or two occasions I was given to understand that some of the members made too much noise on leaving late in the evening. But it was a genuine working man's club, and I mention it to show that such an institution is much more likely to grow and last if it goes upon stern principles of self-support, and avoids the danger of too much patronage and coddling.

The 'St. James's and Soho Working Man's Club,' as it was finally called, has now left its old premises in Rupert Street, and migrated into Gerrard Street. As far as I have seen, however, I must say that on the whole it seems to me a genuine success. The best of it is that it sets an example which working men can follow anywhere if they choose, and that most of the questions, plans, and schemes for working-men's clubs appear to find a solution in the fact of its existence. The club is now contemplating the erection of a new club-house, and on my last visit to it, in Gerrard Street, I was told that it numbered close upon 500 members. If working men do not care to set up a club for themselves in an humble way, and stick to it, no patronage and coaxing will produce anything likely to last.

I have laid the history and rules of our West End Club before a gathering of working men in St. George's, and wait to see whether they take sufficient interest in the matter to establish anything of the kind here. Certainly experience has taught me that, in London at least, the establishment and supervision of a club merely by the clergyman is likely to end in failure. Self-management—with of course such advice as a man of some experience, parson or not, can give, and no set of sensible men will despise—is the only ground on which to go in the conduct of such an institution.

I also learnt a lesson in reference to what are generally understood by 'clothing-clubs,' at St. Luke's. These are supposed to encourage provident habits in the 'working classes' by means of a bonus added to the deposits of such as belong to them. I doubt whether they do, at least with any organic result. Here and there gratifying instances may be quoted of the formation of saving habits by some one who has been tempted to join a club of the kind I speak of by the bonus offered by its charitable promoters, but these institutions,

as generally conducted, are too small and petty in
their principles and regulations to set up any deep
radical action in the social life of working people.
I grant that it is gratifying to the kindly manager
to see a number of poor persons laying by their
pence weekly, and, say at Christmas, to hand back
their small stores in the shape of useful articles,
with the addition of two or three extra shillings-
worth of flannel, or what not, to the bundle which
the depositor tucks under her shawl and carries
off, often with a pleasant adieu, and a remark that
the store comes back 'like a gift.' Exactly. There
is the fly in the ointment. There is the weak
point in the whole business. The result is too
like a gift. Such people would mostly prefer a
present or a dole. They are encouraged in the
sentiment of being recipients of charity. The
little increment to their deposits, so far from
creating or increasing a wholesome sense of self-
reliance, tends, I fear, to nurse that of dependance ;
and, in a healthy state of things, I think that
working people ought to resent this bonus on their
providence. They are willing in some instances
to make use of machinery, such as that of a savings'

bank, to put odd sums away out of daily reach, and to accept an interest which, being commercially calculated, is not degrading. But where this interest arises from charitable contributions they have been found to detect its pauperising influence, and to decline it ; and the fact of such disinclination having been found to exist anywhere casts a suspicion on the good which this charitable increment is supposed to promote. I met with a case in point at St. Luke's. When I first went there I inherited an old-fashioned clothing-club. People were invited to deposit their money, and if they took it out in orders for severely useful articles, which they were directed to get at certain shops, received interest on their deposits to the amount of 20 per cent. ; while, if they simply took back their money, no interest was added. I found this club languid ; there were only 117 depositors. In analysing the thing I discovered that 91 per cent. declined the bonus, and took back at Christmas merely the sum of their deposits in coin. I therefore called the depositors together, and told such as came that the old club would be discontinued, but that if any would like me simply to take care of their money I would begin a penny bank, the members of which should have no interest, and buy their own books. In a few months we had 1,600 names on our list, and the business of conducting the bank became so onerous, that I was obliged to decline the deposits of those who did not live in the district. This set me to question the whole fabric or scheme of charitable bonuses. These have certainly an air of providence about them, and may perhaps be used with least harm in cases where the depositors are members of such an association as a mothers'-meeting, for there they are mixed up with so much else that they lose their distinctiveness. But the mere charitable bonus, though it has an air of providence about it, is little better than a disguised dole, and I am afraid is apt to encourage the very thing from which it is supposed to provide an escape. The money which supplies the bonus, and is publicly subscribed by charitable persons, is, indeed, not paid down to the recipients on the nail, but every recipient comes under the shadow of petty dependance when he or she goes before the 'gentleman' or 'lady' to have a few pence added to the score on the depositor's card. The aim of the true philanthropist should be, not to bribe people into providence by gifts, but to show how small savings really mount up, and thus help to deliver the depositor from any sense of reliance on charity.

Talking of penny banks, I hope that the time is coming when those which at present form part of a clergyman's pastoral economy will be superseded by companies on a much larger scale. I have before me the prospectus of a project, 'The National Penny Bank,' which strikes me as so good that I quote it at length :—

'(1) The object of the Company is to establish Penny Banks, on commercial principles, in London and elsewhere, similar to that which has been so successful in Yorkshire.

'(2) The main wish of the promoters is to encourage habits of thrift among the industrial classes, to extend the facilities for saving, and to manage the business in such a manner as to secure that those in the receipt of weekly wages may use the Bank. The establishment of the 'National Penny Bank,' on a strictly commercial basis, has been determined upon, to prove that the industrial classes do not desire, or in any way need, charitable assistance to provide them with facilities or inducements for saving. At the same time the promoters, beyond providing powers to declare a dividend not exceeding 5 per cent., do not enter into the scheme as a commercial speculation.

'(3) The Yorkshire Penny Bank has been founded about fifteen years. It now holds invested deposits to the extent of nearly 400,000*l.*, and is a strictly commercial undertaking. Its success warrants the promoters in hoping that in London even greater results may be obtained.

'(4) The undertaking is intended to be supplementary to the Post Office, and other Savings' and Penny Banks, but its minimum deposit will be as low as one penny.

'(5) It is intended to make the rules and regulations of the Bank as popular as possible; to bring the Bank to the people; to start branches, wherever it can be done; at workshops and places of business; to avoid complicated and unnecessary restrictions; and, in fact, to carry on the work of the Bank in promoting thrift, in the same way and with the same facilities with which a successful trader in any other business seeks to develope his custom.

'(6) The Bank proposes to facilitate the purchase of Consols in small sums, to promote Life Insurance, both in the Post Office and elsewhere, to make known the advantages of Deferred Annuities, Endowments, and other means of saving, and to facilitate by the machinery of the Bank, which will provide for the collecting regularly of small sums, the possession of such securities by the weekly-waged classes.

'(7) As soon as one thousand shares (of 10*l*. each) are subscribed for, it is proposed to commence business by opening a branch in each of the Metropolitan boroughs.'

This has a wholesome promise about it, but even such a large extension of the present institutions would be much less needed if the meshes of the Post Office Savings' Bank were made a little smaller, so as to catch sums less than a shilling, and the banks themselves were open after working hours. Perhaps this is too much to expect, but at one stroke an incalculable impulse might thus be given to the provident tendencies of the people.

A shilling is a good deal for a working lad—and young people compose the bulk of depositors in the existing parochial penny banks—to lay by at a time. While the stray pence which would reach a shilling are being accumulated they sorely ask to be spent.

Anyhow, in the extension of penny banks without interest, or with only such as is justified by ordinary commercial conditions, I think that one very promising influence is to be found. And the sooner so-called provident clubs, with a bonus dependent on charitable contributions, die out, or are swept away, the better.

Among my failures at St. Luke's I must reckon and mention the really very strenuous efforts I made to improve the streets and dwellings of the district. I do but repeat a truism when I say, that it is hopeless for a clergyman to expect to see highly religious influences at work among people who are incessantly surrounded with degrading circumstances, and the fire of whose life burns low by reason of the tainted air which they breathe. It is very true that drunkenness produces degradation ; but, on the other hand, it must not be forgotten that degradation produces drunkenness. One radical way to raise people and cure them of their intemperance is to remove the causes which minister to their physical debility. In many dwellings, especially in the central and western-central parts of London, one room constitutes the house and home of a working man.

Now I would ask my reader, What would be the effect of this mischievous crowding on themselves and their families? What would your pulse be if you slept in the same small room you had worked in all day, with perhaps your wife and three or four children? If your medical man were to feel it thus fluttering or weak, he would probably prescribe some stimulant. Now comes one cause of mischief. A man wakes in the morning with a bad pulse and no appetite. Nature says, 'Give me something.' So he steps out, or sends one of the children and a bottle, turns up his little finger with a dram, and is relieved. But when a man, with such a spur as the *consciousness of temporary relief* from the use of alcohol, begins to drink in the morning, there is small hope of his recovery, or, at least, he is exposed to sad moral and physical danger. It is very easy for those who have every sanitary appliance, suites of rooms, change of occupation, fresh air, tubs, and well-cooked food, to cry out at the intemperance of the working classes; but this is not a radical vice among them, it is mainly a result of circumstances which drag them down, and if we should judge any severely for its prevalence, we should judge those whose indolence or selfishness permits such a state of things to continue. There is another provocative to drink, in the monotony of trade. Work is now so much subdivided that a man is tied down to the ceaseless repetition of a particular process. Do not suppose that one person makes a pair of boots. A 'bootmaker' does not join the seams; he fastens the 'upper' to the 'sole;' a 'closer' does the stitching. So with a coat. One is 'good' at collars, another at button-holes, &c. Now this wearisome beginning over and over again at the same part of a process so acts at last upon some men that they 'break out,' as it is called. Nature avenges herself; she creates a long-desired diversion by a bout of drinking. There is the alternative, close at hand. You cannot expect every

man to 'clean' himself, and go to the British
Museum for an hour's recreation. There is all-
potent gin, which carries the weary worker off into
its region of delirious change, round the corner, for
a few pence. In a day or two the man returns
to work, with red eyes, shaky hand, and crusty
temper, to create still more rapidly another accu-
mulation of bilious weariness, which he dissipates,
with lessening resistance, by the same miserable
means. There are other influences which we sorely
need. I am really speaking chiefly of my experience in St. Luke's, Berwick Street, and a few of
these current pages are taken, with slight altera-
tion, from an article which I wrote in *Macmillan's
Magazine* some ten years ago, about some of the
ways of working men. I say that there are other
influences which we need. Air—we want more
air. Play—we want more wholesome play. If
those in the crowded parts of West London would
but get out more into the parks, thereby involving
a better dress and a refreshing contact, however
slight, with other society and scenes, we should
hope to check or disturb the creeping palsy of domestic stagnation, which too often results in periods

T

of monotonous toil, relieved by slovenly idleness and drink. The worthy gentlemen, ruddy and pious, who sent up petitions against the Sunday bands from the country would, I am sure, relax much of their indignation at the offence if they knew how hopelessly some of those packed together in central London get mired in depressing drudgery, and how thankful they eventually would be to be tempted out of their close courts by some attraction which such as have green fields around and blue sky above them do not need.

As to the condition of my old friends at St. Luke's, Berwick Street, I am constrained to say that the local remedy they, and some thousands of others in their predicament, most need, is better streets and houses. Efforts have been made from time to time to draw public and parochial attention to their case. These may so well be taken as a sample of others, that I will mention their particular necessities, and in so doing help to serve the battery which is working against all such social arrangements as do mischief to the working class. I use names, for any one who lives in London and reads this may go and see for himself some of the truth of what I say; and those at a distance, who may feel any concern in a local matter which has a general interest for society, will follow and understand me better than if I were to put an imaginary case before them.

The population of St. James's, Westminster, is 35,324, of which one-third, more or less, is lodged in about one-eighth of the space occupied by the whole parish. My own district, as I have said, lay in the most crowded part of this crowded portion, and is stated by authorities learned in statistics to be, by comparison with other localities, the most populous district of its size in London. All the houses in it, with the exception of those which have been already adapted to the requirements of the residents, were built for one household alone; but having been deserted by the class for which they were designed, are now crowded to their chimneys by the families of working people. The rents are high, the buildings old, and the accommodation, in the majority of cases, scanty and indecent. In the thick of the most crowded parts, moreover, there is an additional evil in a number of blind, or half blind courts and streets, which dam up all those influences that are opposed to wholesome commerce and trade. There are the spots where thieves and other persons beneath the more fashionable profligates of the parish assemble. They do not live there, but meet, and more or less degrade the residents. A network of courts, too, is mischievous on sanitary grounds, as well as on social ones. It shuts out fresh air as well as the corrective public eye, and tends to injure the health of the residents, as well as to provide a rendezvous for bad characters.

Any one can see that this, with all its vested interests, and, in many cases, the indifference of the sufferers themselves, some of whom have, I fear, at last grown to like it, is a heavy dragon to fight ; but fought it has been, and will be, till it is slain. Some time ago a long and toilsome protest on my part drew such attention of influential residents in St. James's to this cancer in their parish, that a proposal was made in the Vestry to cut the cancer right through the middle by connecting two streets—Rupert Street and Berwick Street—which run in the same line, the expense being borne by a three-halfpenny rate, and the result being shown, by those who were able to calculate it, to promise eventually a gain to the parish in poor and police rates. All looked promising for a time. I brought leading parishioners to see and smell for themselves. An important representative deputation, with Lord Stanley (now Lord Derby) as spokesman, addressed the Vestry. All agreed that the formation of a new street by connecting the two I have mentioned, and lining the new part with houses well adapted to the working classes, would be a 'boon' to the parish ; but the three-halfpenny rate stuck in the throats of some of the smaller householders who had votes in the Vestry. The larger ratepayers were willing to bear their share, but some, whose share would have been 6s. 2d., looked blue and important. The levels, however, were taken, the cost calculated, and the plans made by an architect. The toil of years came to a crisis in a crowded Vestry. I, having no vote, was advised by several of the leading parochial authorities to do no more. The matter was out of my hands. It was a fair fight. I could not interfere any longer ; so I went to a friend's house at Bedfont, five miles out of town, for a day's rest, desiring the result to be telegraphed to me. It came—I walked out to meet it—in the hands of a little sauntering boy, who threw stones at the birds in the hedges as he dawdled along. The improvement was lost by three votes. Dirt, the great dragon, and six-and-twopence had won that round. The work is still to be done. Then—and I mention this because it bears on one of the most pressing questions of the day—there was a proposal for an underground railway, with a street (in this part of its course, at least) above it, to be carried right through the parochial cancer which the Vestry declined to cure. Fresh interviews, letters, statistics, looking at the place, talking about it, plans, levels, appointments. The old story, now so familiar to me that I think if I were dead and galvanized I should sit up and repeat it straight through. The look of the new street on rolls of paper was to me a picture of Paradise. I could see it as I walked down Berwick Street. Lovely ugly houses in flats, four or five storeys high, with shops on the ground floor, and entresol above, for the shopkeeper to live there if he liked. A common door, with large, well-lit staircase opening into sets of two, three, or four rooms, suitable to the wants of the artisan.

This failed. But I had yet another round with the old dragon of exclusive dirt and needlessly crowded degradation. I really forget how the chance of it began, but I know that I got closer to victory than ever I had done before. The Vestry of St. James's, after another period of debates, and all the wearisome procession of effort which accompanies any struggle to do good, actually agreed to defray half the expense of the projected junction of Rupert Street and Berwick Street by a roadway. The thing seemed to be accomplished. Is it not written in the chronicles of the Metropolitan Board of Works? I well remember, one rainy day, calling at their office and being told that the business was virtually settled, and that notices were about to be served on the tenants of the houses in the obstructive courts. I believe I took off my ha and said a sort of Te Deum as I turned back into Trafalgar Square. But this effort also failed. Vested interests spoiled the carrying out of the scheme in its perfection. The two streets in question are indeed now joined, not by a roadway for vehicles, but only by a wide footpath. The proper work is still to be done. A whole some draught of traffic is needed, unpleasant to the idlers at the public-house corners, in short hair and jackets with thieves' pockets in them, who romp occasionally—in coarse, rough gallantry—with bare-headed girls, thus providing an out-of-door school of foul morals to the children of decent working people. The neighbours complain of these Bohemians bitterly. Poor creatures! one's heart bleeds for them; they—the girls especially—are so defiant of decency. It is a common sight enough. All honour to any man, be he who he may, who can break through the reserve of their close society, and set up a wholesomer action within it. These gentry, who were civil enough to my colleagues and myself, and took in kindness any poor efforts we made to improve them, are ill-disposed towards the police, whose heads they occasionally break with brickbats; and you have only to ask the constable on duty at the bottom of Berwick Street what he thinks of the place, and he will give a character to the neighbourhood which the hard-working residents would resent, since the conspicuous offenders are felt to be a scandal to the genuine artisan, whose business compels him to live near the spot. Indeed they are attracted by

some tumble-down houses close by, where some of
them live ; since they have there the certainty of
cheap rents and the possibility of being able to
run away without any payment for their lodging
at all. But the destruction of any such houses as
they live in would be an unmixed good. They are
mostly bricklayers' labourers, whose work moves
about everywhere over London, and who would be
much healthier if compelled to flit to the cheaper
tenements in the suburbs. A railway through our
district would provide lodgings for the characteristic working classes of the parish, some of whom,
who would be decent in decent streets, sink below
their proper level under the influence of degrading
circumstances.

I am quite willing to admit that changes
which improve the look or value of a place
by driving away the poor who ought to belong to
it, and have tolerable dwellings therein, is cruel,
however it may diminish local expenses. But
in this case, and others, many mechanics who
work and would live in the parish are excluded by the
present state of some of the dwellings, or, if not that,
by the state of the streets in which the dwellings
are situated. And I am strongly inclined to think

that this is true where any nest of foul, close houses is found. Under no circumstances are they fit for human habitation. They breed disease and death, and avenge their existence on those who suffer them to stand, as well as injure such as dwell around and within them. A rotten dirty house is like a piece of carrion. Let it alone, and it not only produces a swarm of its characteristic tenants, but stinks in the nostrils of all who live near it. A rookery – as it is unjustly called, for rooks will never build on a rotten tree, and are conspicuous for their love of ventilation and strict observance of social laws—is by no means a necessary item in the fabric of a city. It is always a sign that a certain portion ought to be cut out, like a fly-blown spot in a carcase. Let us hope that the Artisans' Dwellings Bill will make a clearance in St. James's, Westminster.

Here, at St. George's, we have a street or dwelling-house scheme in hand. I have already referred to the courts of evil repute where Charles Dickens laid the scene of Jasper's opium debauches, in 'Edwin Drood.' The East London Railway has torn a great passage through the parish, on the edge of which lie Perseverance Place and Palmer's Folly, the courts in question. They must come down. I trust to see the day when this chasm opened through the parish will be bordered by improved dwellings, while its centre is occupied by a new street leading down from the Commercial Road to the Docks. I have already devoted much time and pains to the forwarding of this scheme, but at present the condition of the chasm is not such as to allow any reconstruction of its borders. Still I am not without hope, for some time ago I managed to get the representatives of St. George's in the East and Limehouse, which is also concerned in the matter, to meet the Chairman and Surveyor of the East London Railway for an interview with the Secretary of the Peabody Trust. On that occasion the last-mentioned gentleman held out a prospect of the Peabody Trustees being willing to deal with the Railway Company ; and the representatives of the latter expressed their readiness to treat with them in case the financial conditions involved in the matter were satisfactory. To put this tendency into a practicable shape I succeeded in obtaining from the offices of the East

London Railway Company a detailed plan of the lands in this locality at their disposal, and have handed it to the Secretary of the Peabody Trust. Thus, in some measure, the two associations are brought together, and I trust they may be able to do business as soon as the works in connection with the railway are sufficiently advanced. The benefit to the parish would be incalculable. There is no doubt but that new dwellings provided by the Peabody trustees would be appreciated. They have some blocks not far off, in Shadwell, which are filled by the very sort of people who need them most.

Our Medical Officer, Dr. Rygate, in his report for 1872, in speaking of the extension of sanitary care in St. George's, remarks on the low mortality in model lodging-houses, which is only 14 per 1,000. He adds elsewhere, in his report published in 1874 : 'Dwellings for the poor might be erected of a better character, by placing more power in the hands of an active local or general board, with greater and cheaper facilities for the purchase of property ill-constructed or kept, and the erection on the land of properly ventilated and drained, and otherwise well constructed edifices, occupying no more ground than those removed, but extending in the only other fit direction, namely, upwards. Such dwellings would let well, and would be a great saving to the rates, as many would have their *amour propre* raised by living therein, and thus be kept off the relief list. Thus a parish could afford to pay a fair price for such property, and be satisfied with a moderate interest. Looking at the subject in a broad view of it, there could be little doubt of this, and with the great local experience of the members of the parochial boards, such purchases might safely be left in their hands.'

This reads well; and as Mr. Hardy's Artisans' Dwellings Act has come into existence since it was written, I trust that our Medical Officer of Health will be encouraged to further the application of some of its provisions in St. George's, whether the Peabody Trust moves in the matter or not. We have a great chance now from the clearances caused by the construction of the East London Railway; and there are divers other parts of the parish where the new Act could, with the concurrence of the local authorities, be made to produce excellent fruit ; for though, as I have repeatedly remarked, our poor people have more room than those living in the central or west-central parts of London, their houses need much improvement.[1]

I have said that the worst courts skirting the route of the East London Railway lie just beyond the eastern end of the parish churchyard ; and it is in connection with this that we are trying to make another highly desirable improvement. Our long disused churchyard is of considerable extent, covering, together with the church and rectory, some three acres of ground. This is already planted with trees, and a large portion of it, at the eastern end, is comparatively bare, of tombstones. Our lilacs and laburnums this year made quite a respectable show, and the vines in the churchyard are hung with grapes. But it is practically inaccessible. There are people who have lived close by for years who have never even seen it. It is surrounded by high walls, and is readily available only to the residents in my house. An avenue of small lime-trees in it is indeed called ' The Rector's Walk '—I

---

[1] Since writing the above I am delighted beyond measure to find that our Medical Officer recommends the removal of between 200 and 300 houses in the Parish of St. George's as unfit for human habitation, under the provisions of Mr. Hardy's Act.

suppose from having been the pacing-ground of some predecessor of mine. It would be difficult to adapt the western portion of the ground to public use, as it is crowded with tombstones, brick graves and vaults, but the bare eastern part invites transformation into a public garden. There is no such garden near. There is no spot nearer than Victoria Park, some two miles off, where a working man can sit down and rest himself under a tree, or children escape from the gritty streets. I have told the parishioners that I shall be very willing to yield my privacy so far as to give up this open space to them, if they will put their hands into their pockets and make a bright and accessible spot of it. There would be great risk in the mere turning of Ratcliff Highway into the churchyard as it is. It must be properly fenced; and one great feature of our scheme, which involves the formation of a public path that should traverse the garden, would be lost if an attempt were made to utilize it by admitting the public into the spot as at present circumstanced.

We see, however, a way to use the place which would provide such use of and access to it as would hinder it being possibly employed as a questionable hiding-place, as it might become if only one narrow way of approach were made to it by opening from the Ratcliff Highway a court which leads towards the churchyard.

The burial-ground, now also disused, of the Wesleyan Chapel in Cable Street, adjoins that of the Parish Church, and is well planted with trees. It is, however, separated from it by a gaol-like wall, high spiked and strong. The obvious course is to throw all sectarian reminiscences to the winds, pull down the middle wall of partition between the two burial-grounds, and thus provide a good acre or more for a well-ordered public garden, traversed by a broad path between two of our main thoroughfares, Ratcliff Highway and Cable Street. This would make it easily accessible to all the parish, bring the watchful eye of the public into it, and also provide a new and pleasant access to our three chief buildings, the Vestry Hall, which looks on the Chapel burial-ground, the Chapel, and the Parish Church. There would be an additional advantage in the path, inasmuch as it would lead towards the new station to be built on the East London Railway, some hundred yards or so from the Chapel.

I am happy to say that the Vestry have taken up the project with spirit, and that there is good hope of our seeing it translated into fact. Great things are expected by some of us from our public garden, though I think people hardly realise the effect which will be produced when the horrible high spiked wall between the dead Churchmen and their deceased Nonconforming neighbours has been pulled down. Its demolition will shed a special sense of space into the centre of the parish. And I hardly dare to picture to myself the final result when a good acre or more is laid out with flower-beds and lawns, and well dotted with groups of shadow-casting trees, under which people can sit, away from the hot and gritty streets. My imagination, moreover, constructs a fountain in one particular spot, with a pool around its base, where bright-winged waterfowl will circulate and convey the contagion of refreshment to the wearied eye by the appetite with which they will enjoy themselves in the spray. I hope, too, we may have our colony of tamest pigeons, and it will go hard if we cannot get a few peacocks to unfold their stores of colour in some part of our garden. Indeed the place is capable of being made a delicious protest against and escape from the monotony of griminess which broods over miles upon miles of dull straight streets, where the granite stones of the road and the long lines of hard brick house-front are broken by no better plea for green growth and life than is seen in a flower-pot on a window-ledge, or a lark imprisoned with a handful of sod and a heart full of song. The united burial-grounds have, too, the additional capacity of being converted into a living retreat, since they are skirted by high walls, which can be covered with ivy and Virginia-creeper. Thus the eye as it glances under the trees and across the lawns and flowers will be stopped by no reminder of the dusty town, but rest finally on leaves. This will make our garden seem larger than it would otherwise appear. The sense of space will be further encouraged by the absence of many high buildings in its immediate vicinity. As it is, the top-gallant masts and pennons of the big ships in the Docks mark the sky line from some parts of the churchyard.

But I must not anticipate too much. These lines which I now write will have to be finally committed to type before a spade can be struck into our soil or a stone of the gaol wall between the burial-grounds pulled down. And there is such a thing as a slip between the cup and the lip. We have, however, taken such serious steps for the erection of the public garden, that I hardly think we shall fail. In the first place the idea is by no means a new one. It has crossed the minds of divers of our residents before now. And when once, not long after I came to St. George's, and was looking, with some of my leading neighbours, out of a back window of the Vestry Hall upon the two burial-grounds, and said something about the recreative capabilities of the place, my remark met with immediate response. After the matter had been the subject of many stray conversations with leading fellow-parishioners, I ventured to call a public meeting of the inhabitants in reference to the scheme. It was well attended, and the favourable words of the speakers met with unanimous acceptance. The meeting issued in a numerously signed petition to the Vestry to take the project into their serious consideration, and a strong recommendation of it by the local press. Many difficulties

of course arose, and were discussed. Legal opinion was taken on our powers in respect to the
churchyard. Once the line of our progress was
apparently worn to its thinnest thread ; somehow
or another the project was on the point of being
abandoned *sine die*, in the hope of its promoters
being able to take it up again when public opinion
on the matter had become more matured. A
member of the Vestry then made a promising
remark, and, I, being in the chair, asked him if he
would like to put it into the shape of an amendment.
He did, and it was carried. Then a committee,
including our two churchwardens and myself, was
appointed to go more fully into the matter. We
took considerable pains, and at last brought up
to the Vestry an enlarged and well-considered
scheme, with estimates, down to the provision of
a lawn-mower.

After much discussion this was unanimously
adopted, with the understanding that no steps
should be taken to acquire the Chapel burial-
ground till an answer to a memorial had been
returned by the Metropolitan Board of Works,
who, we imagine, will help us with some 2,000*l.*,

the half of the money needed to carry out the scheme. I am pleased to see that the decision of the Vestry, adopting the report of the committee, has met with the decided support of the leading local papers, both Liberal and Conservative ; and I cannot resist the utterance of the feeling that, if the parish finally carries out this scheme, much will be done not only to make a desirable improvement in its midst, but to show that St. George's in the East is not behindhand in public spirit, and its appreciation of 'sweetness and light.'

At present the matter awaits the concurrence of the Metropolitan Board of Works. It was laid before them at the close of their session this year, and—I write in August—will probably be decided one way or another not very long after they meet again in October. Let us hope that the long escape which the members of the Board have it in their power to make from the dust and crowd of London, will help them to hear with kindly ears the prayer of those who, having had through the hot autumn months little or no relief from the monotony of the streets, will then crave help in the provision of an accessible and shady garden by such time as the summer again makes grass and flowers precious to the Londoner. Our garden, if judiciously furnished and laid out, will bring into our midst just one of those touches of refinement which the East, and especially this part of the East, needs, and in which it contrasts most unfavourably with the the West and other suburbs of the metropolis.

It will moreover, if made, fit in opportunely with the improved streets and dwellings which must eventually replace those which stood on, or now partly skirt, the ground that has been broken up in the formation of the East London Railway. The importance of a more commodious passage through this part of the parish is becoming more distinct as the large steam-ferry across the Thames at Wapping seems likely to be established. This ferry will involve a very great increase of traffic through St. George's—for Wapping is a mere strip, a few yards wide, between us and the river—and a broad street, parallel to Cannon Street Road, will be needed towards the more eastern districts of these parts. Facilities for making this obviously appear in the demolition of houses caused by the East London Railway. Indeed the whole question of the reconstruction of this part of the parish is radically affected by this projected ferry. There seems to be every prospect of its success, and it will have much the same effect on us as a new bridge. Vehicles will converge to it from the whole district east of the London Docks, as well as from the surroundings of Rotherhithe on the other side of the river. Now there are forests of masts for miles in the Docks on either bank of the Thames, representing ships laden with merchandise which must mainly reach or be forwarded towards its destination by wheel and axle ; but at present there is no such communication between these stores of goods and adjacent manufactories except by London Bridge. A waggon must turn at least three miles out of its way if it wants to pass from us to our very close neighbours whom we can see walking about on the Surrey side of the Thames. It is indeed impossible to calculate the effect which a large steam-ferry will have upon the traffic of these parts, for it will not only relieve that which is now imperatively compelled to go round by the bridge, but probably create much which it has hitherto not been worth while to attempt. The real need of an improvement, especially of one which promotes facility of intercourse between sections of busy people, cannot be known till it is made.

In looking at the social, moral, and religious prospects of St. George's, it is plain that such an advance in the provision of decent dwellings for the working classes as is rendered possible by the present railway clearance must raise many who are now depressed. Though the poorest and least reputable court anywhere has generally some witness for God and order among its inhabitants or households, a better house generally makes a better home. It brings such as live under its roof within the reach of, or nearer to, those influences which descend. It lifts, or helps to lift them, into that stratum of the community that respects itself. How can we expect a poor uneducated man, strained with toil and surrounded by such depressing facts as foul walls, rotten floors, a leaky roof, and stinking drains, to have energy and moral courage enough to keep himself and his belongings clean?

The family which, in despite of adverse circumstances, raises itself, or accepts higher influences, inevitably moves into a better house, or renovates that in which it is compelled to live. But put even a decent family into a pigsty, and it will most likely contract some of the habits of pigs. Compel a man to wear rags, and he will be exceptionally strong if his moral character does not become tainted with squalor. Now a ragged and dirty house is a sort of family suit, or livery of ill fame, and has something of the same effect on the household as a compulsory foul dress would have on the individual.

What chance have the ministers of righteousness and order in their efforts to raise those who are thus weighted and degraded? Here and there one may be lifted out of the slough, but the real righteous work is to do away with the slough ; and every step in the improvement of the poorer sort of dwellings is one in this hopeful direction. I desire to do all honour to the efforts which are made by outdoor services and sermons in 'low' neighbourhoods to reach and revive the degraded ; but, after all, the most practical street preaching is a pulling down of foul degrading habitations.

In respect to our pastoral work at St. George's
I have little more to say. We have the usual
machinery. Our mothers'-meetings are well attended. Our infant-nursery, which has been established and is supported by one kind Lady, meets
with growing acceptance, and I think helps to set
up here and there a wholesomer domestic action
among those for whom it is intended. We have
moreover, a kitchen, whence we aid some sick who
need the assistance of the cook as well as that of
the doctor ; and we are fortunate in being furnished,
owing mainly to the liberality of one person, through
the London Nursing Society, with a trained nurse,
whose business is mainly to go about and show
people how the sick may be best tended, lending a
hand here and there, looking in to see that the sanitary direction has been attended to, the medicine
punctually given, the bandage, blister, or poultice
properly applied. It is a homely, but most useful
labour ; and if any one likes to take part in a
distinctly good work, he or she may send a donation to the London Nursing Society. We are
fortunate, too, in the kind services of several ladies,
who not only look after the details of the kitchen,

the mothers'-meetings, &c., &c., but, going about, help to cheer many a poor soul. Along with the machinery and these ministrations we have a weekly meeting of a branch of the Charity Organisation Society, held in St. George's, and, in co-operation with it, are strenuously anxious to avoid giving such aid as tends to pauperise the receiver. We try as far as we can to help people to help themselves.

There is one branch, however, of pastoral work which we have hitherto been unable to see established. I mean a retreat or provision for such of the poor harlots who haunt some of our streets as desire to forsake the life they lead. It is of little use holding midnight meetings for them, and urging them to repent, if no means are provided for their exit from the vicious circle in which they move. There ought to be some main Refuge or Home for these poor women in this part of the East of London, and divers small accessible receiving houses which would act as first doors of escape. These should be simply equipped, but there should be some known roof under which a harlot, touched with weariness of or shame at her condition, might be sure to find a Christian motherly woman who would take her in without reproaches, and give her lodging till she could be moved on to the Chief Refuge, whence she might be, perhaps, restored to her own home, or put in the way of a respectable start in life. In time past some unfortunates have sought an escape from life in death. There is a bridge in our Docks over deep water, whose surface is greasy with droppings of tar, and where dirty chips float lazily about, from which some have leaped in a spasm of disgust and despair. On the outer wall of the riverside police stations may be seen occasionally some such dry printed announcement as this :—'Found, the body of a woman, unknown ; age apparently 25 ; linen marked " Mary." '

We ought to do something more than we do for possible penitents ; and I, for one, should be glad to take part in a well-organized scheme for their reception and recovery, and I know of several who would join us in the attempt. But such a scheme would need careful preparation. The experience of those who have had much to do with penitentiaries establishes the fact that there is deplorable weakness of purpose and perversity of

action even amongst such as have had moral
courage enough to apply for protection and deliverance. In many instances they seem to have
lost the commonest sense of truth, and the influences
which should be brought to bear upon them must
be not only pure, but strong. They need, especially
at first, the closest and firmest supervision. Thus
in divers cases it has seemed best to the good
people who seek their salvation to subject them to
severe ecclesiastical discipline. I am inclined,
however, to think that a homely and natural treatment is more likely to recover them of their sin,
and rekindle a life that has been marred by habits
of drunken sensuality A kind, firm manner, which
does not display the Christian spirit that underlies
it by insistance on minute ascetic regulations, would,
I think, judging by the broad experience of
humanity, be more likely to heal the weak and
wounded soul than the sudden and severe subjec-
tion of the penitent to an importunate routine of
religious services. The treatment employed should
of course not be marked by mere human pitying
good-nature ; it should be, and claim to be, deeply
divine ; but there is danger lest the recovery of the

sinner should be checked by very strenuous demands for her frequent use of stated devotional exercises.

If we ever see our way towards the provision of a Refuge for this part of the East of London, I trust that it will be managed with the deepest Christian tenderness and the firmest Christian strength, but without a prominent display of ecclesiastical machinery. The establishment and conduct of such an institution demands, indeed, the most delicate and persevering care, but I do not see why, by the combined action of those in these parts who mourn over iniquity of the kind I mean, something effectual could not be done to provide an escape for such as may be willing to seek deliverance from the evil they are beset by, and the grievous state into which they have fallen.

It would lead my pen on over too many sheets of paper if I were to pursue thoughts which arise in considering what better means could be devised for the good of those who suffer in any way, and how the means now existing could be better used. Throughout the land there is, however, obviously a growing belief that any attempts to heal the sores

of society must be based more on an enlarged
perception and combined use of the great laws of
life which God reveals than on the most manifold
and strenuous but scattered individual charity. The
action which has of late years been set up, and
which characterizes the Social science, Christian Philanthropy, and Religious Enthusiasm of the day, is
marked by a tendency to rest upon deep principles
and adopt wide schemes.   Educational, sanitary,
and ecclesiastical measures all go to show this, and
when such as are of an age to do so compare the
state of things with what they can recollect of it,
even so lately as five-and-twenty years ago, they
must, I think, be cheered by the thought that in
these respects at least a better day is dawning upon
East and West London.

LONDON : PRINTED BY
SPOTTISWOODE AND CO., NEW-STREET SQUARE
AND PARLIAMENT STREET

www.ingramcontent.com/pod-product-compliance
Lightning Source LLC
Chambersburg PA
CBHW031041120726
47905CB00007B/2265